6 99

STRAND PRICE
$ 15<u>00</u>

LOST NEW YORK

NATHAN SILVER

LOST
YO

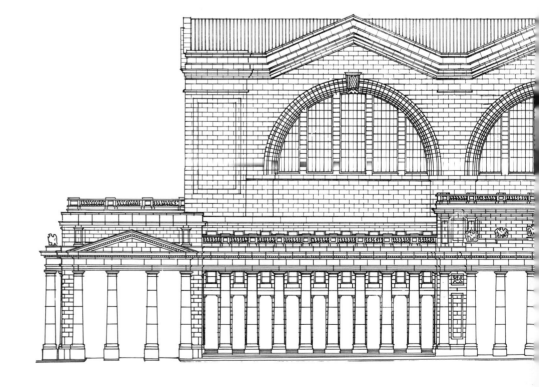

NEW
RK

WEATHERVANE BOOKS
NEW YORK

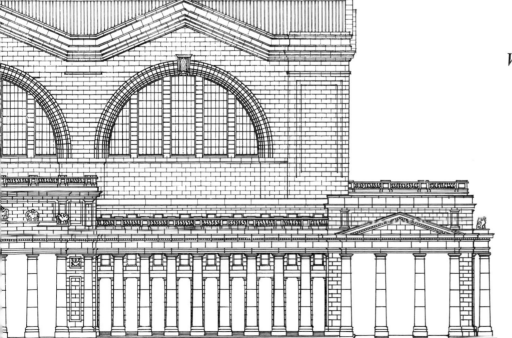

Copyright © MCMLXVII by Nathan Silver
Library of Congress Catalog Card Number: 66-11220
All rights reserved.
This edition is published by Weathervane Books, a division of Barre Publishing Co., Inc.
by arrangement with Houghton Mifflin Company
a   b   c   d   e   f   g   h
Manufactured in the United States of America

ACKNOWLEDGMENTS.   This book would never have been begun if the funds for the original exhibit had not been made available by the Columbia University School of Architecture. Gratitude is due the entire Architectural Staff and Faculty, particularly David E. Glasser, Raymond Lifchez, and Dean Kenneth A. Smith.

While I was seeking photographs in archives and picture collections, the following people were most helpful: Adolph K. Placzek, Librarian of the Avery Architectural Library at Columbia; Hedy Backlin and Richard P. Wunder of the Cooper Union Museum; James J. Heslin, Rachel Minick and the late Arthur B. Carlson of the New-York Historical Society; Romana Javitz, Curator of the Picture Collection, New York Public Library; Vivian Hibbs of the Metropolitan Museum of Art; Henriette Beal and Albert K. Baragwanath of the Museum of the City of New York. Others who kindly helped me find pictures were Margot Gayle, Ernest Emerling of Loew's Theaters, Col. George F. Johnston (ret'd), Stanley D. Katz of Cushman & Wakefield, and Mrs. J. DeW. Peltz of the Metropolitan Opera Association.

No picture book about New York buildings could be written without relying on the pioneer works of I. N. Phelps Stokes and John A. Kouwenhoven. Alan Burnham's book *New York Landmarks* has a bibliography on New York architecture which was most useful.

Many of the photographs in this book were taken by just a few photographers, whose interest and devotion in recording old New York buildings made their recollection possible. Among these were the Wurts brothers, the Byrons, H. N. Tiemann, Berenice Abbott, and Samuel Gottscho. Their work has my greatest esteem and appreciation. The quality of almost all the photographs printed, many of which needed retouching and special treatment, is due to Modernage Photo Services in New York, and Harry Amdur's special attention.

Some of those who offered advice, information and help during the writing of the text were the successive Executive Directors Prof. James G. Van Derpool and Alan Burnham of the Landmarks Preservation Commission, Henry Hope Reed, Jr., of the Municipal Art Society, Stephen Zoll, and William Blackburn. Joan Stoliar and Betsy Smith patiently answered many of my questions about typography and layout. Joyce Hartman of Houghton Mifflin not only edited the book, but coordinated the gathering of late material and arranged complex schedules while I was living abroad. Jennifer Keen, John Grimshaw, Stephen Morant, Roger Stonehouse, and Philip Green read some material and made valuable suggestions. Bette Mahoney, Colin St. J. Wilson, and Rhoda Brawne read the introduction in an earlier form, and offered cogent criticism. Commissioner Evelyn Haynes and Mrs. Regina Kellerman of the Landmarks Preservation Commission and Mr. Baragwanath read the entire book in manuscript, generously sharing their expert knowledge of New York. None of these people are responsible for my judgment and errors.

My wife Caroline spent a beautiful spring indoors, researching, retyping and tirelessly reordering the book. My greatest debt is to her.   — N.S.

To my Father, who grew up on Broome Street (page 206)

And my Mother, who met him uptown

CONTENTS.

PREFACE.

This book began as an exhibit at the Columbia University School of Architecture.

By 1963 it seemed urgent to make some sort of plea for architectural preservation in New York City. It had been announced that Pennsylvania Station would be razed, a final solution seemed likely for the 39th Street Metropolitan Opera, and the commercial buildings of Worth Street were being pounded into landfill for a parking lot. I suggested that the collective picture of some vanished first-rate architecture would make a sobering reminder of how much finer a city New York could have been with its all-time best buildings still intact. With the help of the staff and faculty of the School, the show was then planned. We wanted it to be an editorial for preservation, and also to support the growing local awareness that some legislative protection was needed for many urban landmarks.

I began to look for photographs of old New York buildings in archives and picture collections. What had at first seemed a relatively simple, closed-end research job proved to be a vast undertaking. Thousands of buildings deserved to have their likenesses rescued from oblivion. Often, ones I thought of showing had poor or no photographs available. Some of the photographs were unidentified — with not only their architects unknown, but even their uses and locations in the city obscure. Moreover, it soon became clear that, just as a city is more than a collection of buildings, *Lost New York* had also to take notice of other things — the old places of recreation, the working districts, the tenement neighborhoods, transportation systems, and the parks.

When the exhibit opened in January, 1964, it was still a work-in-progress. Yet the response was stimulating — and the remarks rather unexpected. Typical comment (mostly from architects and their families, at that) was not "too bad this was lost, it was beautiful," but much more often, "too bad this was lost, it was old." The commonest assumption was that I was arguing the justice and worthiness of preservation *for the sake of the past*.

Yet there was some confusion somewhere, because the typical landmark-preservation response to a need for the past has been, "let's have legislation to save the few monuments that matter." For example, in a recent article on preservation, Alan Gowans, of the University of Delaware, had this to say:

> Almost any building has historical associations for somebody; almost any building manifests some style; almost any building is a delight in somebody's eyes. The result is that, generally speaking, whenever any old building is threatened with destruction, for whatever reason, there is always somebody ready to defend it . . . The only effect of operating on principles that justify saving everything is to make 'preservationist' a synonym for 'obstructionist' in the minds of developers and planners . . . *

---

* Alan Gowans, "Preservation," *Journal of the Society of Architectural Historians*, October, 1965.

But this attitude would stop discussion just where it should start. *Why* is someone always ready to defend an old building? All we have to account for it and describe it is that unsatisfactory word "nostalgia" — psychologically a probably very interesting concept. In 1964, it seemed to me unconscientious to disparage its basis. Perhaps nostalgia has a most important and useful component, and that is why this book went on from the Columbia exhibit.

Now, after a far broader search into New York's past, I believe that while the objective of *preservation* may be, as Professor Gowans puts it, the "survival of the fittest," this explanation of objectives doesn't make clear why some things not terribly fit in the history of art or culture still should be maintained. This is discussed in the Introduction. And then there is Gowans's point that "the basic question to ask in deciding on preservation is not what visual pleasure and intellectual significance given buildings have for us, but what they had for the generation that built them." This truly takes preservationism away from ordinary people and turns responsibility for it over to architectural historians, where I am happy to leave it. But it seems to me that *conservationism* is an equally vital and more challenging concern of ours, as pages 18–20 try to explain. If architecture is, as I believe, not the art of beautiful buildings, but the art of human use, then conservation of good use is a matter of concern for everyone, in the present and future, and conservation is not "obstructionist" but wise. That is the point of this book, and the aspect of *Lost New York* best remembered.

A small final statement of extenuation and expiation. No New Yorker should be surprised by how quickly things change. This is true even of personal beliefs. Perhaps unvarying opinions form an animus which tends to crack on a vast and obdurate subject, like a hammer which breaks before an anvil does. In the future I hope to take further account of some notions, hardly suggested here, about designing for specialization and generalization. I recently came across at least one book (Richard L. Meier's *A Communications Theory of Urban Growth*) that I wish I had read before I wrote my own.

As some of my attitudes have changed mildly, some situations have changed radically over the course of the several years it took to choose pictures and conduct research. Important decisions affecting New York were made by city administrators, planners, and landlords. During the many months that it was necessary for this book to be locked in production limbo, the text was not accessible to the latest news, such as the implications of laws passed by the preservation-minded 89th Congress.

It's risky to adopt the double intention of recording both history and the up to date process of history, but in this book it still appeared essential to note the mechanics of changing situations, in order to get at the subject of change itself. Even if change is likely to change, a serious current appraisal, in planning or writing, would seem a matter of common and intrinsic responsibility.

Cambridge, England

LOST NEW YORK

. . . I am with you, you men and women of a generation, or ever so many
      generations hence. . . .
What is it then between us?
What is the count of the scores or hundreds of years between us?

. . . I too lived, Brooklyn of ample hills was mine,
I too walk'd the streets of Manhattan island, and bathed in the waters
      around it,
I too felt the curious abrupt questionings stir within me.

     – Walt Whitman, *Crossing Brooklyn Ferry*

The business lunch took place at the Plaza, an excellent first-class hotel
of the old type. I like those vast and handsome hotels which are not at all
in modern style but which have acquired a past through their richness and
substantiality. There are living pasts and dead pasts. Some pasts are the
liveliest instigators of the present and the best springboards into the future . . .

     – Le Corbusier, *When the Cathedrals Were White*

Architectural
survival
Cities reveal as much about time as about place. They usually start from small settlements which grow
and change at first in a direct response to site conditions, climate, and available materials. This corre-
sponds to the fundamental task of architecture — to protect man from the tyranny of nature. As a
settlement becomes better established, building typically turns to the development of institutions. An
orderly pattern for these is the second great task of architecture, and once a settlement has reached this
point, it can no longer be called a primitive or pioneer place. The settlement, growing and changing,
next takes up forms that clarify the livelihood, culture, and communications of the inhabitants, and meet

the needs of an expanding population. Urban geographers can look at plans of such human settlements and determine many facts about the people who live in them. The question of what they are seems to have something to do with how long they have been in one place.

If a settlement is left to change as it will, the ever more complex requirements of life soon make it lose its initial clarity. In modern cities, the many paths and purposes of the inhabitants eventually generate subtle and non-architectural facilities (the conference room instead of the meeting hall; the telephone instead of the market square). The city then becomes free to adapt itself to ephemera, and most have done so. The pervasive sights of most cities at present are stoplights, billboards, parking lots, unrelated shop-fronts. Some urban theorists, such as Kevin Lynch, have argued for a return to the "imageability" of the city when its paths and purposes were simple. Others, such as Jane Jacobs and Herbert Gans, have maintained that modern life is too complex for planned clarity in cities to be desirable or even possible.

Quite outside the thesis and antithesis of this debate, something recognized by all parties is how satisfying old buildings can be. When seen in the context of growth and change, there is no mystery about why this should be so. An old building is usually one that has continued to make sense in its relationship with both its place and its users. The building's survival through time — this *alone* — is a circumstantially strong indication of its value. If time is a dimension that clarifies and enriches things, the conservation of such buildings would seem worthwhile.

To provide a basis for opinion about the buildings shown in this book, some notes on architectural survival seem appropriate. In the case of New York (as of any city), history provides strong indications of what is likely to be useful and meaningful. The notes therefore start with characteristics of New York's essential formation, including the peculiar New York qualities of common experience. Then they go on to the significance of the past for its own sake, and forces and proposals that naturally operate for change. They conclude with present municipal powers with respect to architectural continuity, and prospects for the future. This is all meant to provide a dialectic for discussion about the vanished architecture shown here, and how it was most valuable. But it is also hoped that these notes will suggest some logical ways of reappraising the need for continuity in the urban environment.

I.   The colony is now established on the Manhates, where a fort has been staked out by Master Kryn Fredrycks, an engineer. It is planned to be of large dimensions . . . The counting-house there is kept in a stone building thatched with reed; the other houses are of the bark of trees. Each has his own house. The Director and commercial agent live together. There are thirty ordinary houses on the east side of the river, which runs nearly north and south . . .

François Molemaecker is busy building a horse-mill over which shall be constructed a spacious room sufficient to accommodate a large congregation, and then a tower is to be erected where the bells brought from Porto Rico will be hung . . . The houses of the Hollanders now stand outside the fort, but when that is completed they will all repair within, so as to garrison it and be secure from sudden attack . . .

When the fort, staked out at the Manhates, will be completed, it is to be named Amsterdam.*

The choice of New York was an accident of water. Its geography provided a harbor and afforded natural positions of defense both at the passage of the Narrows from the lower bay and at the Hudson estuary. Although one of Europe's "most memorable occurrences," the settlement of New Amsterdam was done in a matter-of-fact fashion by the West India Company. Manhattan was bought and paid for, buildings were staked out and built. This was all odd to the Indians, who knew nothing of ownership of the land. They had sold the right to inhabit it, to hunt and fish and cultivate the soil. They themselves would have moved on in case of drought or bad hunting. The Europeans brought to the New World their own ideas about possession and property, their assumption being that building was more significant than land. The most important aspect of the new settlement therefore emerged at the very start, when the new occupants showed that possession of the land meant permanent ownership and that the new community was to be there to stay.

Manhattan soon had many settlements on it which slowly grew together: the Bowery, Sappohanican (later Greenwich Village), Harlem, Manhattanville, Bloomingdale, and Inwood. These were villages, rural agricultural centers scattered over the island, connected to the separate small town of New Amsterdam at the southern tip. According to a plan of 1660, New Amsterdam itself had only about 300 houses, which stopped at Wall Street. Streets divided the town into about twenty blocks. The shape of the town layout was related to three main features: to Fort Amsterdam, a palisaded fort south of the present Bowling Green with four salient points; to the Heerewegh (later Broadway), which ran north; and to a canal where Broad Street is now.

First growth   By 1670, six years after the English had captured the town, a boat basin had been constructed on the East River side, a market had been built on piles over the water, and a slaughterhouse constructed outside the town wall. In 1696 the first Trinity Church was built. The tower of Trinity and the polygonal cupola of the first city hall were New York's most outstanding landmarks. Stepped-gable buildings were giving way mostly to timber adaptations of English houses. About the same time, walls of many of the stone houses began to be marked with iron date numerals in consciousness of age.

The Manhattan settlement had been set up by the Dutch to serve as a trading center, and trade remained its fundamental purpose through the English colonial period. An act of 1680 gave New York millers the sole right throughout the province to grind and bolt flour. Prosperity grew so greatly as a result of this law that, while it was only in effect for fourteen years, the population of the town tripled and the number of buildings and city revenues more than doubled during that time.

By the middle of the 18th century the old wall at Wall Street was down, streets beyond were being routinely added by survey, and landfill operations were taking place around the perimeter of the island. The meeting of the Stamp Act Congress in New York in 1765 demonstrated that the city had become not only a trade center, but an important political center of the colonies as well. After the Revolution it became the first federal capital. When Alexander Hamilton became Washington's Secretary of the

---

* From *Historical Narrative of All the Most Memorable Occurrences Which Have Come to Pass in Europe*, an account by Nicolaes van Wassenaer, published in Holland in 1626. This translation is from *Mirror for Gotham* by Bayrd Still, N.Y.U. Press, 1956.

Treasury, his Bank of New York was a means and part of the plan to put the country on a firm postwar financial basis. New York's financial leadership was to remain pre-eminent among American cities.

After the Revolution a kind of monumental architecture was regularly appearing. Some important commissions given to Pierre Charles L'Enfant also signaled a change to French-oriented taste in building (see page 90), just as there had been a change from Dutch to English style almost 100 years earlier. Vernacular construction remained about the same: mostly timber buildings, with stone and brick construction largely downtown and for wealthier people.

The growth of the city and increasing value of downtown land required the building-over of natural land features. The Collect Pond, a fresh water lake north of what is now Foley Square, was filled in 1803; a few years later the hills that had made it a basin were leveled. The Mangin-McComb City Hall, New York's architectural masterpiece, was incompleted but in use in 1811. From it issued the Commissioners' Plan, a map eight feet long which plotted future streets up to 155th. It showed an absolutely geometrical gridiron of rectangles (except for Broadway, too familiar to be changed). Nothing like Central Park was proposed, but small park-squares four blocks long were staggered at about twenty-block intervals. The rectangular geometry was familiar. Such patterns in towns had been built as early as the 5th century B.C., and they had straightforward advantages: good economies of usable land due to the conventions of rectangular building; convenient location-finding with only two directional "fixes," the minimum requirement; a simple traffic situation on the streets at each intersection (at least for travel at the speed of horses; T-shaped intersections would have been more suitable for faster vehicular traffic).

Planned growth

It is probable that aesthetic considerations, apart from those related to economy and hygiene, carried little weight with the New York commissioners. In this they were not different from planners of the Renaissance, who, according to Siegfried Giedion, were also disinterested in the unity of the straight avenues they built.* But it would be unfair to condemn gridiron plans as lacking possibilities. The design principle of the street in perspective has found an effective response on many streets in New York where cornice heights and building facades are coordinated. (The English planner Lord Llewellyn-Davies has called these facades on linear streets New York's "endless architecture.") On the other hand, a linear street can have a section-by-section series of relationships structured by the street, like individual beads on a chain. There is more of this kind of diversity, charm and sensibility on 55th Street, for example, than in many medieval towns.

However, the main problem of gridiron plans is that they are unrelated to the natural terrain, and with their dogmatic patterns tend to obliterate land features. In New York, the Commissioners' Plan of 1811 must bear full responsibility for this. Only the fact that the planners anticipated nothing but garden suburbs for the endless blocks helps explain a design which prophesied (and has become in some parts of New York) a frighteningly monotonous sea of city.

New York building is not only a question of *why*, but *how*. The kind of construction, the building-plan types in commonplace use, the notions about spaces inside, the decoration favored — these are all building characteristics, and in the texture of the city the slow development and change of building characteristics is the nub. It is also a quality of the city's essential formation, since the productive variety of these forms is an accumulation of single decisions related to many individuals.

Early building

---

* *Space, Time, and Architecture*, Harvard University Press, 1941.

New York's building designs can be most rewardingly studied in the varieties of houses and commercial buildings. It is instructive to look beyond Federal or Greek Revival decoration to the more essential changes which affected the quality of life within. In New York row houses, for example (pages 128–137), there is the relocation of the staircase from the back, where it reduced light and air, to the center of the hall, allowing extra windows for rooms instead of the stair. Or there is the change from pitched roofs with dormer windows to flat roofs with more headroom on the attic floor, which corresponded to the development of satisfactory asphalt and cheap metal roofing techniques.

From the 1830s on, many of the lofts put up for warehousing and the textile trades were miracles of refinement, lightness, economy and grace. There was nothing like them elsewhere in America (not until later). Prefabricated specimens were even sent abroad in the 1850s. If anything should forever stand as a radiant image of the essential New York, it ought to be the commercial buildings — the ones built on straightforward systems of bays with iron ties, the cast iron fronts, the wide open glass walls, the primitive lifts improving in design as loft succeeded loft — the Eccentric Mill Works, Harper's, Stewart's (pages 166–168). The uniqueness and significance of these buildings and the historical development of the light industrial type mark their participation in the city's early growth. Later types of building, the skyscraper for example, found their highest expression elsewhere, even if New York built the most. But the best and purest that New York can offer are the commercial buildings which were formed as a perfect response to contemporary needs, in that hour of inspired invention.

The first park   Though small squares were shown in the 1811 Commissioners' Plan, parklands were left out. They cost money, were associated with private gardens of the European aristocracy, and interfered with land speculation (they were also called potential nests for criminals). Since all these things were true, the advocates of Central Park had to overcome many such objections before coming to terms with the natural one: the fact that the selected site was a wasteland. The park squares of London were often groves and gardens preserved intact from noble estates, but there was no equivalent site preparation in the case of New York. Until the 1850s, the city was built only up to about 42nd Street. In 1850, the area from 59th to 110th Streets and Fifth to Eighth Avenues contained scrubland, farms, squatters' shacks, and reservoirs for Croton aqueduct water. The decision to build a great park there was partly aided by the availability of relief workers in the 1857 Depression, although that came after construction of the park was under way. The magnitude of the project was undoubtedly more an expression of the linear nature of New York's growth, led on by the cheapness of land to the north.

Frederick Law Olmsted's park is twice as large as Regent's Park or Hyde Park in London, and only Dublin, Vienna and Paris have bigger ones. In its landscape design, it is all that Humphry Repton ever proposed for an English country estate. There was even a sheep meadow, like the working pastureland within English estate gardens. As it came to be built, the basic New York topography of outcropped rock still shows through, but such ancient configurations as McGown's Pass of Revolutionary War fame were swept away. The construction of the park cost $16,500,000, a vast sum at the time even for so vast an undertaking.

The design was remarkably beautiful and remarkably artificial, in the sense quoted by Repton from Burke: "No work of art can be great but as it deceives. To be otherwise is the prerogative of nature only." Central Park's richness and variety should be understood as essentially an artistic and artificial effort, in order to appreciate the delicate balance of elements that was established between wild and controlled parts, open vistas and densely planted sections. The growing up of the city around the park in later days has therefore enhanced rather than detracted from the magical artifice of the design. The greens and copses with the city skyline beyond make the park effectively a middle-distance phenomenon, allowing no chance of mistaking its perfect form as mere countryside. The backdrop of buildings also makes the enormous two-and-a-half by a half mile size of the park visually clear and understandable in terms of human scale. 150,000 people can be within it on a pleasant summer day, but the park is artistically a miniature for all of that — a tiny image of nature. Its original layout has been seriously compromised quite recently (see page 39), but Central Park remains the greatest example anywhere of English landscape design, a major art, and the most essential of the fundamental elements of the city.

The passage of time has made more emphatic most of the early tendencies of New York's foundation period. The city became the financial and managerial headquarters of the country, and, as the principal American port, the immigration center. Many of the immigrants stayed and provided cheap labor for a generation, supplying industries with workers while bankers offered risk capital. New York's garment industry is one of the permanent survivors of this period, and the mechanics of the situation still work today.

Emerging characteristics

New York was not only closest to Europe by being a great port, it also tended eastward by sharing some European manners and European social divisions. Henry James called the first Waldorf-Astoria the "characteristic" of the city, though the characteristic in 1904 might more easily have been the poverty and misery and crime that Jacob Riis reported. As a cosmopolitan community, however, New York took on the social and cultural eminence of a European capital, eliminating Boston and Philadelphia from contention by the end of the 19th century. The lack of a national political center in the country's largest city only underlined New York's preoccupations as clearly differentiated from those of the American heartland.

Financial and cultural forces acted together to form the theater and film industries that were based in New York, and these eventually helped provide the liberal backing and audience that encouraged writers and painters and dancers to live and work there. After World War II, the permanent location of the United Nations began to give the New York international life some focus, and perhaps at last the Waldorf-Astoria (the new one, this time), with its residence of the U.S. Ambassador to the U.N., became a New York "characteristic."

New York's essential formation is only part of what is unique about the city. If what matters can be measured by common experience, there are familiar attitudes toward some of the physical realities of New York that can be read as clues. These are ordinary things, real or imagined, that are "known" — a sort of city psychology, a New York *thing*. The architect Louis Sullivan (in his 1901 book *Kindergarten Chats*) knew that New York had a characteristic mentality that was very different from that of Chicago.

The experience of New York

One of the more immediately sensed aspects of New York is its economic richness and fatness — the dignity of capitalism, often expressed in architecture. This was as essential an ingredient of Pennsylvania Station (page 32) as it is of the new Chase Manhattan building. Both these places seem to ring true for New York, because the spirit of the city is within them.

The garment industry and the buildings that housed it are also places clearly expressing New York things, as are the downtown canyons between skyscrapers, and also the districts for amusement, from the Tenderloin of old days to the present theater-lined 45th Street. Then there is the current equivalent of vernacular building: the aluminum and porcelain store fronts, the Coca-Cola ads over delicatessens, the new aluminum double-hung sash in tenement windows. This much is ephemeral, but it ranges over to absolutely essential characteristics such as the brick and the brownstone, the sheet metal cornices and cast-iron railings of row houses, the old granite curbstones and block street paving, the vanishing shepherd's crook lampposts.

All the commonplace, prevalent building materials and familiar methods and practices contribute to the urban fabric and the experience of New York things. Every detail matters. It is important to perceive that hardware stores are often painted orange out front, and that the color of newspaper kiosks and shoe shine stands is green.

Some of the *imagined* things about New York are also fundamental and important. The fact that it is "a melting pot," for example; the fact that the sidewalks are "paved with gold." Horace Greeley must be remembered (he reputedly said go West, but he stayed in New York); and the heroes of Paul Goodman's *Empire City* and Nathaniel West's *Miss Lonelyhearts*. Also Alfred Kazin as *A Walker in the City*; and O. Henry, Edith Wharton, F. Scott Fitzgerald and the Plaza fountain. The ideas of New York that are present here — though some are romantic or largely imaginary — have become part of New York experience, even to distant strangers who have only heard about them.

There are a great number of New York things, "characteristics" in the Henry James sense. Many of them are very vague, special, not perceptible or not common to everyone, but they are still knowable and valuable (though they are emphatically not all *visual* things). The most significant of all New York things may be that there are so many different paths and aspects.

The significance of the past

II.   Like any place else, New York's essential characteristics are rooted in times past. There appears to be good reason to believe that people take special notice and gain special strength from familiar surroundings. They seem to respond to the past in a somewhat consistent, if uncritical, way.

The smallest elements of the physical world are the first external things important to babies. Data about surroundings is gradually learned, with the first things often remaining the most precious. The child's toys, his bed, the pattern of cracks in the ceiling may be memories that will never leave him. The Dutch architect Aldo van Eyck calls attention to the place of the doorstep in meaning and remembrance. It is physically insignificant, yet it is the link between the hearth and the world. Again and again one crosses it and returns to it.

Movement along familiar streets is accomplished by proceeding from perceptual detail to detail. The most elemental things seem to be recognized first. There are streets that one knows from the slope of the sidewalks, though one can't remember what buildings are there. Memory and familiarity are sequences of trifling impressions, like corners, steps, doorjambs. They constitute the mechanics of experience. Architecture, when it is at its best, arouses the spirit and methodically organizes these impressions.

In addition to normal perception and awareness of surroundings, there are ample grounds to believe that all people are conditioned by certain incunabula of cultural and individual orientation. Sir James Frazer's *The Golden Bough* has explored the myths and superstitions that seem to underlie much of primeval experience. Jungian psychology is concerned with the common symbolic elements of existence. The great landmark ideas of Ernst Cassirer based an entire philosophy on the meaning of signs and symbols, one that has been in the mainstream of thought since about 1925. It is clear that man is not rootless, but has long taps back into time.

People value old things, not just for their rarity as antiques, but for their history of human use. They are moved by the gouges and dents in a library table, the smell of an old pipe, the comfort of old clothes. But not only use is significant — the hidden relationship of things to us is very important. People are fascinated by their own family histories. They will travel thousands of miles to walk the streets where their grandfathers lived. The smallest details of the relevant past are a testament, as Marcel Proust knew. In *Remembrance of Things Past* a man's being is shown by a revelation of his total expenditure of time, explained through the description of vivid scenes at particular places, with full details given. Combray, one of Proust's places — nothing more than a landscape and some familiar things — turns out to have the greatest power to explain and recreate the people who lived there.

In his 1964 book, *The Eternal Present*,* Siegfried Giedion is concerned with questions of the significance of the past to our own period. He finds that it has " . . . become apparent that human life is not limited to a single lifespan but goes far beyond. It is as impossible to sever its contacts with the past as to prevent its contacts with the future. Something lives within us which forms part of the very backbone of human dignity: I call this the demand for continuity."

If continuity is as basic to us as Giedion believes, then there must be more to nostalgia than sentimental longing. We may find within it secrets about who we are and where we came from, last week or a thousand years before. Some of these secrets about our lives are disclosed by every corner of a familiar city, soaked in meaning and memory. But architecture itself is freighted with the greatest temporal meaning. This is because it is *devised* to consolidate the necessities of a time, in a place. John Ruskin, in *The Seven Lamps of Architecture* (1849), gave as a key element of his architectural theory "the lamp of memory."

Architecture depends on development through time in order to be clearly related to society and culture. All that is really meant by a building's "style" is that is it more or less understandable in terms of time. The greatest buildings are practically radioactive with history. Regardless of how old or new they are, they tell a true story of life, since they were devised to serve and symbolize human use. An encounter with magnificent architecture irradiates even someone alienated and disaffected. In *You Can't Go Home Again*,† such is Pennsylvania Station for Thomas Wolfe:

> The station, as he entered it, was murmurous with the immense and distant sound of time. Great, slant beams of moted light fell ponderously athwart the station's floor and the calm voice of time hovered along the walls and ceiling of that mighty room, distilled out of the voices and movements of the people who swarmed beneath. It had the murmur of a distant sea, the languorous lapse and flow of waters on a beach. It was elemental, detached, indifferent to the lives of men. They contributed to it as drops of rain contribute to a river that draws its flood and movement majestically from great depths, out of purple hills at evening.
>
> Few buildings are vast enough to hold the sound of time, and . . . there was a superb fitness in the fact that the one which held it better than all others should be a railroad station. For here, as nowhere else on earth, men were brought together for a moment at the beginning or end of their innumerable journeys, here one saw their greetings and farewells, here, in a single instant, one got the entire picture of human destiny. Men came and went, they passed and vanished, all were moving through the moments of their lives to

---

* Pantheon Books, Inc.
† Charles Scribner's Sons, 1940.

death, all made small tickings in the sound of time — but the voice of time remained aloof and unperturbed, a drowsy and eternal murmur below the immense and distant roof.

The past is important because a sense of continuity is necessary to people — the knowledge that some things have a longer than mortal existence. Affirmation of this can be sought in nature and art. Cities, as the greatest works of man, provide the deepest assurance that this is so. They do it in individual ways, so as to be meaningful to many, by revealing and asserting the sometimes hidden mysteries of their being. Cities are places where different styles converge and mix. As a cultural manifestation, this may be a city's greatest function — its ability to present the full record of the past. Lewis Mumford put it most succinctly of all: "In the city, time becomes visible."

Forces that alter the city

While cities must adapt if they are to remain responsive to the needs and wishes of their inhabitants, they need not change in a heedless and suicidal fashion. It is therefore worth looking at the way some unplanned forces for change operate, to see whether they sometimes work against the needs and wishes of many citizens.

Repair and neglect

The most common force of change is deterioration and replacement, most frequently when buildings undergo repairs. Some buildings in the world are over a thousand years old, but the elemental construction materials of which they are made — stone and tile and heavy timber — are still in the slow process of deterioration. When deterioration is very marked, it is usually because negligence has allowed necessary repairs to accumulate. Perhaps the building has outlived its usefulness and a completely new building is anticipated. In rental properties — and most of the buildings within American cities are in this category — it might be expedient for an owner to neglect his property, hoping to draw off his rents and sell to someone else before too long. In New York, where patterns of discrimination and some housing shortages still exist, this sort of temporizing quickly leads to conditions of drastic disintegration. Tenants realize that the condition of their lives only affects their landlord in the size of his rent rolls, and therefore have no reason to feel that his house is theirs. Where other forces (such as a scorched-earth planning program) may become operational, the landlord need only wait for his property to be officially called part of a slum, and then reap further rewards when the building is acquired for clearance.

Fashions in land values

Most city buildings are destroyed in order to be replaced by larger buildings. Land values in central city areas are forever on the rise. But land values must be considered not only according to solid worth. There are also matters of social selectivity, prestige, and other things that work according to fashion, and New York has some of the most fashion-conscious real estate in the world. In 1965 it was possible to buy a five-story house, twenty feet wide, in fairly good shape and with decent architectural character, on an attractive street, at the following prices: $15,000, $27,000, $60,000, and $125,000. It was only a matter of whether it was located in the Lower East Side, Chelsea, Greenwich Village, or the Upper East Side. For the most part, fashions were dictating prices. These fashions have currently led property east of Central Park to become much more valuable than similar property west of the park. The odd thing is that at the time they were built, the row houses west of Central Park were mostly the finer, single-family buildings, while those east were largely unpretentious houses planned for several families.

When fashions in real estate are as marked as they are in New York, dense rebuilding takes place rapidly in order to get as much income as possible from a good address. In the case of Sutton Place, Lower Fifth Avenue, Washington Square, Gramercy Park and a large part of Greenwich Village, opportunistic redevelopment to exploit fashions has all but obliterated whatever substantial virtues were once present in these neighborhoods. Often the very buildings which helped set the initial character are replaced.

Private transfer of property is almost always governed by limited objectives, which may be contrary to general objectives such as the public welfare. At present in New York almost the entire urban environment can be disposed of as private owners wish. In contrast, medieval guilds protected towns against unreasonable and unnecessary change, often by controlling title to the land. The existence and disposition of every building was a matter of public concern, and sound use was therefore imperative.

Expendability and property

It also happens that modern technology and advanced architectural understanding can provide highly refined and particularized buildings, if not yet freely expendable ones. The availability of this talent for specialization acts as a catalyst toward change, especially since there is often a real need for specialized accommodation. Building users no longer have to be satisfied with general-purpose spaces when architects can give them new buildings that are individual as well as flexible.

Specialization

The modern implications of these questions of expendability and property seem clear. With changing user needs, land of high value, free powers of change in private hands, and ready accessibility of the means, the demand for the ever-increasing expendability of architecture is inevitable. And the onslaught for change must first affect the most venerable buildings in town.

More inevitable economic forces come into play because of the expanding requirements of society in management operations. The corporations, institutions and government offices located in New York are constantly seeking more space as their responsibilities grow. They need to provide for more people, with more complex jobs, communicating more efficiently. And meeting this problem is in fact the crux of a city's operation. These organizations must expand or perish, and since the contribution they make to the urban situation is vital, no city administrator would prevent them from expanding, or force them to move elsewhere to do so.

Requirements of management

Unfortunately, management organizations are made to compete for living space not only with each other, but with different vital facilities of the city — an unequal battle. The unrefined use restrictions of New York's fire codes and zoning laws seem effective in barring law offices and painters' studios from areas designated as residential, but they haven't withstood the pressures that forced Park Avenue between 45th Street and 59th Street into commercial occupancy. In that complex change, fashion made a residential area become commercially desirable. Once the encroachment of offices had begun, no attempt was made to conserve any of the centrally located housing, or even to encourage housing and offices to exist side by side as in European cities. The city cooperated by permitting zoning to change from residential to business use. The very high land values, created by fashion, rebuilt the whole section as offices in a few years.

Changing social and urban values also make for inevitable forces that alter the city. Reasonable demands of the city's inhabitants for greater amenity are now constantly being heard, ever more reasonably. If it is finally deemed proper for the city to have small park-squares every few blocks, some big questions of demolition will have to be weighed in the balance. The land adjacent to park-squares would thereby greatly increase in value — perhaps enough to pay for the tax and property loss.

Changing cultural values

Fresh social and urban values may lead to more community centers, more places of public assembly and leisure. Except for borough halls and county courthouses and the like, the outlying city districts lack almost everything worthy of civic pride or community attachment. Now almost *everything* must be sought in midtown Manhattan.

Museums and libraries must still largely depend on private charities to support them, and have not expanded because of the limits of their resources. The city universities have not grown much. These are all latent but potentially active forces for change in New York, still waiting for new cultural values to find them.

Planned change

Planning is necessary if a city is not to remain static, locked forever in the 18th or 19th century, unresponsive to the modern and future needs of its population. A full discussion of modern planning theory would be out of place here — there have been whole books about the Federal Urban Renewal program alone — but the subject deserves brief comment, because vast changes in cities are occurring increasingly as a result of full-scale planning, though not vast in New York so far.

Many planning theorists have written on the form and nature of the city, in attempts to explain its workings and improve its qualities. It often happens that discussions about improving the functional workings of the city lead immediately to proposals for an ideal new city form. Such discussions are more suited to new cities than existing ones. Undoubtedly a few revolutionary planning theories have been brilliant and influential — Ebenezer Howard's, for example. But frequently the result has been that some *revolutionary* schemes have been swallowed in part by *existing* cities, whatever the intentions of their authors.

The most famous revolutionary theorist, and one whose intentions were perfectly clear, was Le Corbusier. The full model for his ideal city was to be built over Paris. Hating the chaos and dirt and disorder, he designed a Radiant City to take its place. Huge buildings would be set vast distances apart in great parks. The streets of the city would have infrequent intersections to permit cars to move at rapid speeds between buildings. The "front door" of each giant house would admit hundreds or thousands.

Le Corbusier wrote a book about New York, *When the Cathedrals Were White*.* When the cathedrals were white, he said, men had built with fresh vision. New York inspired him to think of his Radiant City again. The height, the gridiron of streets, the promise of change excited him. "New York is not a finished or completed city," he wrote. "It gushes up. On my next trip it will be different." The vision followed him home, and back, again and again, in 1920, and 1926, and 1928, and 1939. "I cannot forget New York, a vertical city, now that I have had the happiness of seeing it there, raised up in the sky." Unlike Paris, there was no lack of industry, and no reluctance to experiment. "New York has such courage and enthusiasm that everything can be begun again, sent back to the building yard and made into something greater, something mastered! These people are not on the point of going to sleep. In reality, the city is hardly more than twenty years old, that is the city which I am talking about, the city which is vertical and on the scale of the new times." When he looked for a moment among the towers, he was impatient with what he saw: "Between the present skyscrapers there are masses of large and small buildings. Most of them are small. What are these small houses doing in dramatic Manhattan? I haven't the slightest idea. It is incomprehensible. It is a fact, nothing more, as the debris after the earthquake or bombardment is a fact." There was no need to be held back by this. "A considerable part of New York is nothing more than a provisional city. A city which will be replaced by another city."

Yet from time to time, somewhere amid the enthusiasm and impatience and revolutionary fervor, there appears the other Le Corbusier, the humane witness. For page after page he goes on about sweeping away the past, then suddenly is distracted by something that suggests continuous existence. He takes the measure of the people that he sees and declares them ready, if any ever was, to sweep away the dead past; but in the next breath he praises the architectural spectacle and historic sensibility of the bronze statue of

---

* Reynal and Hitchcock, 1947.

Washington on the Sub-Treasury steps, in front of a Doric porch, in the canyon of Wall Street. One Le Corbusier hates the half-heartedness of it all, the only *provisional* Radiant City. The other Le Corbusier is enchanted by the accident and diversity of building. "A hundred times I have thought: New York is a catastrophe, and fifty times: it is a beautiful catastrophe."

When the Cathedrals Were White is a most compelling example of a revolutionary proposal for city change. No consideration detains the author's impatience to sweep away and begin again. The splendor of the necessary acts of destruction are almost magnificent in themselves — small wonder that some planners find ruthless change fascinating. Yet I believe that every idea is false except the perhaps essential one: that the principle of adaptation exists in the place itself; that, as he said, "the new times will discover the law of tomorrow in the furnace of cities." What Le Corbusier sought and found in New York was a fundamental principle — one of the New York things. His discovery was that New York is the city that should have been and perhaps yet will be the white city in the sky foretold by its history. But the crux of the matter is whether his proposal is the apotheosis and justification of that history, or the destroyer of it.

III. All city change in New York is monitored, if not exactly regulated. Government powers exist not only in overt planning, but covertly influence every property decision. New York has powers of taxation, building codes, fire and health regulations, zoning laws, rent control laws, planning procedures, and preservation policies (now supported by law). Most of these are established in terms of restrictions rather than requirements, but in practice they move building and real estate in certain directions. For example, since buildings are currently being appraised for taxation on the basis of how prestigious they are, rather than on the basis of their actual value (as revealed in an appraisal of the Seagram Building*), it is obviously public policy to reward undistinguished building, a lesson not lost to speculative builders.

Building codes and fire and health regulations are primarily established to protect life and promote safety. By setting up inflexible standards they can also eliminate certain economical possiblities and force other action. Some stirring examples of how these codes may influence a city's form can be seen in New York. The water towers on almost every roof and the fire escapes, which are virtually a New York trademark, are creatures of these codes.

Building, fire, and health regulations

Zoning regulations are designed to advance the general welfare of the community through an overall system of land controls that protects the usefulness and value of property, and that tries to promote orderly community growth. New York's original Zoning Law of 1916, one of the earliest in the country, was

Zoning

---

* A few years after it was built the owners of the Seagram Building, Park Avenue between 52nd and 53rd Street, discovered that New York City was assessing their property for taxation as though the entire street floor land was covered with building and earning rent. Seagram took the matter to court, claiming the open space was a plaza and a civic contribution. The court upheld the city. It found that Seagram either planned the open space for prestige, or was demonstrating poor business acumen; and in either case the city was entitled to taxes based on the hypothetical full development.

replaced by a completely new law in 1960. The earlier experience had indicated how valuable a tool good zoning policy might be. The new law was an attempt to bring controls up to date.

Both old and new Zoning Laws deal with building use, bulk and area. The *use* to which a parcel of land may be put is obviously a matter of public concern, if a slaughterhouse or a chemical factory is not to appear next to an apartment house. The *bulk* is important if good light and fresh air are to be maintained for the adjacent property and streets. The *area* of the land covered by building is important for similar reasons. When zoning law was based primarily on requirements of health and general welfare and elimination of nuisance, these principles could not be faulted. But the new law, encouraged by recent court decisions permitting zoning for aesthetic purposes, has tried to legislate for civic beauty as well.

Since the old *bulk* requirements were bringing about "ziggurats" and "wedding cakes," complicated tiered buildings that just fit the "envelopes" of prescribed daylight angles, the new law established calculations for determining allowable bulk that encouraged the building of sheer slabs, presumably more tasteful shapes. (This was in post-Lever House days. It might never have happened if the artful setbacks of the Daily News or RCA buildings were still fresh in the mind.) To make sure that speculative builders played the game, the new law encouraged them to set back their towers from the street, and for compensation could add to the bulk by other complicated formulae. In the new law, the street setback is known as a "plaza." These setbacks are the reason why the present section of Sixth Avenue in the Fifties looks so uncharacteristic of New York. The new towers there — in imitation of Seagram, but unlike it — stand in very uncertain relation to the avenue, violating the strong lines of the streets with their "plazas." They create no real spaces as they upstage each other. They and the buildings overhead contribute nothing to the linear nature of the avenue, the "endless architecture" that is one of New York's greatest visual strengths. Sometimes buildings should be walls, not towers. The new Zoning Law encourages otherwise.

In the new area requirements for buildings, large scale projects are heavily favored. In order to get any allowable area to build upon that makes economic sense, several of the old New York land parcels must usually be assembled into one site. This means, for example, that a typical brownstone row house is now obsolete in New York's zoning. It couldn't be built in midtown under the new law, because it would cover too much land — too great a percentage, and would be hemmed in by other regulations invented to fit larger properties. But very much taller residential buildings could be built, provided several old brownstones parcels are assembled. Far more dwelling units than there were in the old brownstones can be built on the combined lot under the new law. The scale of building — and the relationship of building to street — would have to change. Needless to say, such a proposition promotes the acquisition of many small properties such as brownstones, with great profit incentive for their clearance and replacement.

Rent control   The most insidious force for destruction in New York has been the Rent Control Law. Whatever the merits and justifications for setting standard rents, the fact that a free rental market is permitted to exist alongside the controlled market has caused New York to lose, and will make it continue to lose, some of its most distinguished and essential architecture.

The present Rent Control Law is now administered by the city, but it is a descendant of national wartime price controls. According to the law, housing and commercial rentals in most buildings over a certain age are fixed, subject to board review. The rentals can be increased up to 15% upon change of tenancy, or because of increased services, or if the landlord is not getting at least a 6% return on his investment. They can be decreased if services are decreased. In a situation where there is not enough housing to go around, such a law is worthwhile, since it protects tenants from inflated rents and safeguards their occu-

13

pancy. Even under the present circumstances, when city housing has become less scarce, the law still preserves the stability of communities, and a social balance among people of different incomes is maintained by widely different rents within the market.

The law has often been criticized; not only by real estate groups, but also by disinterested observers. Some feel that the law should be changed because communities have become *too* stable; for example (a much-heard example), older couples will usually hold large apartments after their children have left home, simply because their continuous tenancy maintains their low rent. Others believe that the law should be abolished or gradually eliminated, since an unregulated housing market is somehow "better" than a regulated one. The wishes of these last critics have been fulfilled, causing the unmitigated disaster that has befallen some of the city's best buildings.

Besides the buildings under Rent Control, there were always some not controlled at all. At first they were only those accommodations — never in short supply in New York — which were very expensive. A free market existed in that rarified air. But upon pressure for gradual disengagement from controls, all *new* building was kept out of Rent Control. It was thought that since the new buildings would have to compete in rents with controlled ones, their rents would stay down during the period of transition. But what in fact has been happening, with impeccable economic logic, is a sort of Gresham's Law of building — bad buildings are driving out good. Any new cheap construction can command higher permitted rents than better buildings formerly in the same place. Thus commodious town houses are being demolished to make way for economy apartment buildings, because a floor in the former produces less rent than a flat in the latter.

Since the early 1950s, whole sections of New York have been transformed by such new building. Developers have been buying up rent-controlled properties as fast as they can, all over the East Side and the Village and wherever they think the neighborhood might support far higher rents. They tear them down, and in their place cheaply constructed "luxury" apartment houses soon appear. To keep the costs of total rents within rational limits, apartment sizes are minimal. A socially disproportionate number of "efficiency" apartments and one-bedroom ("4-room") apartments are crammed into a typical building.

This is not the building program that the city needs. If the Rent Control Law continues to exist in the future, it ought to include all buildings and it should serve merely as a set of limits which prohibits a drastic rise in city rents. Since the Rent Control Law has excluded new construction, the only question now is how long it will take before all the old New York buildings are down. As long as the law provides that they are in the way of profit, it is just a matter of time.

While the City Planning Commission and the Department of City Planning are nominally responsible for promoting good order in the city, many other agencies have exercised some of the same powers. Among them are the Department of Marine and Aviation, the Traffic Department, and the various borough presidents' offices, inside the municipal government; outside it there are the Triborough Bridge and Tunnel Authority, the Port of New York Authority and the Tri-State Transportation Commission. All of these except the last (which is at present restricted to planning exclusively) are engaged in practical operations as well as theoretical proposals. Since even such city departments as the Board of Education, the Department of Parks, and the Department of Water Supply may plan and build on their own, it is easy to see how disordered the New York planning process can get to be. In the past, crucial decisions were often made to suit whichever agency had the most influence with the mayor. Other times, several agencies would be in conflict, and each would act autonomously. And then some of the most far-reaching decisions, affecting basic city form or calling for substantive settlement of questions of public policy, have

*Planning
authorities*

14

been put over by the independent Authorities or have been agreed upon by the city administration without consulting the electorate. It is obvious even to its present practitioners that planning by conflict and competition among parties which have their own vital interests to promote, done with as much secrecy from the public as possible, is the very worst way to plan. The fact that it has led to irrational change and needless destruction of the city's form is also obvious.

The preservation law
Since 1965 New York has had a Landmarks Preservation Law. The law provides that a Landmarks Preservation Commission may from time to time designate city Landmarks, and that no Landmark thus designated can be demolished or altered on the exterior without the consent of the Commission. Some procedures are mentioned in the law for financial aid in cases where maintenance of a Landmark interferes with an owner's profit. Purchase by the city is suggested if no other assistance is enough. With this law, New York joined over seventy other American cities which had already enacted municipal preservation legislation.

At the time the law was passed, about 750 individual Landmarks were being considered for protection, based on a Commission survey of the five boroughs of Greater New York. A few score have since been designated. The Landmarks are mostly "monuments" rather than buildings of unpretentious character, but some whole districts are additionally listed, such as sections of Brooklyn Heights, Greenwich Village, and the cast-iron commercial area.

At this moment it is hard to say what effect the law will have on checking wanton destruction. It is a good law, strong because its policy is based on governing powers rather than compensation. The theory is that a Landmark is part of the public patrimony, and an owner need not be bribed to preserve it. However, the problems of economic distress are recognized and compensation for such is suggested.

There are two major flaws in the preservation law. One is that it deals entirely with external appearance. Many buildings are far more significant in their interiors — Grand Central Station and the 39th Street Metropolitan Opera, for example. Preservation for such as these ought to be based on maintaining the interiors as well. The other flaw is in the nature of a last-minute insertion in the bill under enactment, a "moratorium clause." It provides that Landmarks can be designated only at three-year intervals, a gaping escape hatch for shrewd wreckers.

Early reaction to the law has been severe. Many institutions, such as the New York Stock Exchange and some church groups, find themselves embarrassed to be owning Landmarks, with some of their property rights now under regulation. Several of the first Landmark designations certainly suggest that the Commission is unafraid of protest. But by failing to designate the old Metropolitan Opera House (see page 226), they have indicated their willingness to be swayed by the most familiar of objections: those made by owners who arrange to sell in order to rebuild. Having made a lucrative deal for the old property, the Metropolitan Opera Association was determined to have no interference from anyone. They didn't want the building any more, nor did they wish any other opera company to inherit it, so for their part, it had to be torn down to provide a site for an office building, and a sum of money for the not bereaved opera trustees.

Application of powers
The fact that many government powers have been used in the destruction of much of New York's essential form doesn't mean that these powers should be abolished or curtailed if preservation is to be more successful. But proper application of powers is everything. If they are contradictory, arbitrary or misapplied, the blind force of legislation and police power are more destructive than *laissez-faire*. They are forces that suicidally increase the self-destructive nature of a modern city, beyond the random injurious acts of the accident-prone.

If considerations of continuity and a sense of the past are to have influence, then there must be someone with the responsibility of determining what things are essential to the city. Measures should be taken to conserve those things from the vicissitudes of heedless change. In New York, concern about the form of the city is obviously part of the jobs of many people, and yet none has particular responsibility. The City Planning Commission is not responsible for *carrying out* plans, and in any case even their wishes may not be followed by the mayor. While the Triborough and Port Authorities do build what they plan, they have bondholders to serve, whose interests do not necessarily coincide with those of the public. The Landmarks Preservation Commission is by law empowered to preserve. But a few score monuments are not a city. If these are all they can hold on to, it is obviously no safeguard against heedless change.

The main responsibility should, however, be that of planners. A planner must be concerned not only with what changes, but with what must not change. Consideration of the second is often forgotten. It is the harder part of a planner's responsibility. The practice of planning, in drafting offices far from the situation, makes it easy to forget about what is to remain. It is easier to create form than to adapt it, easier to ignore possibilities than to struggle with them. It is actually even easier to change than not to change. But when circumstances seem to compel change, this is the moment when the designer has to carefully reflect. Is the corrective necessary?

If a dozen separate agencies control building in New York, and among them can't guarantee the preservation of New York's essential form, then it may be time to attack policy-making by specialists. For want of clear *general* thinking, some urgent and fundamental considerations have obviously never been directed to any of the specialists' offices. But this failure of initiative may be partly a good thing. It is timely, before New York planning overhauls itself and becomes cooperative and efficient, to remember that many of the things planners have been called upon to decide are not matters for experts at all. Preservation and the limits of change are general matters of broad import, which the public at large has every right to discuss. (The explanation often heard for concealment of plans from the public is that full exposure may drive up property prices — a shockingly meager excuse, considering government powers of eminent domain.) An Authority should not have the autonomous authority to decide that eviction of people from their homes is necessary to facilitate some work — as happens now. A great deal could be said about the new "displacement" approach of much public planning, and the sort of disordered lives, neighborhoods, and social systems it is likely to produce. But such problems would not come up so frequently if the people concerned, according to every definition of democracy, were being consulted.

Once the general goals of the city and proposals for comprehensive adaptation are openly debated in the community, the city planner's technical job could begin. Being responsible for continuity, he would have to make the detailed decisions about conservation and change, within the guidelines established by the public policy. Since he would be under a more directly democratic procedure he would be unable to resort to sweeping clearance and upheaval techniques, and his work would become much more complicated and difficult than it already is. Many stages of development would need to be set, and the parts planned for the remoter future might have multiple alternatives. The very complexity of his task would suggest some immediate conservation policies.

This could be done on the basis set down by Sir Patrick Geddes in his 1915–19 reports on Indian towns.*

---

* *Patrick Geddes in India*, edited by Jacqueline Tyrwhitt (London: Percy Lund, Humphries & Co., Ltd., 1947).

16

Geddes believed that to disregard tradition was a vulgarity. He called for "conservative surgery" as an economical approach toward change, condemning the policy of sweeping clearances.

The English architect planners Peter and Alison Smithson were faced squarely with the same question conserving the essential city — in a 1962 study they made of Cambridge. Cambridge University was not only the center, but the basis for the town's growth and continued existence. Yet the lives and work of many people were unconnected with the University. In putting down some general thoughts arising from a consideration of Cambridge, Alison Smithson contemplated the multiple paths of people's lives, the sometimes striking limitations of planning in being able to select, order and define, and the incredibly strong patterns of life structured by forms of the past. Here she writes not primarily of Cambridge, but of all cities:

Conservation could have a real freeing power in our cities. By conserving intact for periods of ten, twenty or forty years such areas that still offer viable human environment — even if its exact nature is indefinable in administrative terms (no more definable than 'the right smell') — there could be established 'fixes' which would cut the field of action for creative planning down to manageable size. The conserved area-fixes would be continual reminders of the right scale of thinking, elucidating at all stages the elusiveness of 'good environment.' Area-fixes would tend to channel creative planning into areas whose environment has been totally invalidated.

In between such areas of conservation and areas of strict guidance forming new environment might then come defined areas neither worth conserving nor clear yet in which way they could usefully be replanned. These might be free of certain planning control for periods of twenty, forty or eighty years, to become experimental areas in which the forces at work could play an ultimate programming role.

Such aids to comprehension of the actual task also allow concentration of available intellect, capital and energy into special areas . . . An open system, one not aimed at a levelling off environment, could make better use of the truly different talents people possess.*

Preservationism   A name that can be given to one kind of limited protection of a city's essential form is *preservationism*. Within its meaning, monuments are considered for their historical value or their architectural importance, but essentially for their own sake. The building becomes the issue of importance rather than its uses. It must be defended as an *object*. The New York preservation law takes notice of Landmark sites, but they are defined and defended in relation to the Landmark itself. It also seeks to protect "Historic Districts." Even though these are environmental rather than individual, appearance and not use is what matters. They are designated as Historic Districts because they have special character or special historical or aesthetic interest, *and* because they represent one or more periods or styles of architecture. In other words, whole Historic Districts are also determined solely by the importance of the buildings as objects. By selecting them as objects, only the external aspects — literally and figuratively — are being defended. Their appearance is preserved by protecting "exterior architectural features."

---

* *Team 10 Primer*, edited by Alison Smithson (London: Standard Catalogue Co., 1965).

Economic survival is sometimes very difficult for Landmarks. The uses of the Landmark and the entire district may change, or may have already changed. Whatever the economic chances for maintaining a historic building when the use remains the same, those chances are usually much reduced when the original use has disappeared and the environment has radically altered. New York's "Old Merchant's House" on East 4th Street is difficult to preserve, if only as a museum, because the old, elegant residences of nearby Lafayette Place (now Street — see page 131) have been supplanted by commercial lofts. The district even lacks the vitality of that kind of use, for not many appreciative visitors come by.

Whatever the reasons for cherishing them, many of the most valuable elements of a city are those buildings which are wonderful for their own sakes. They may be so bound up with the city's history, or so representative of the spirit of a certain time, or so beautiful as buildings alone, that their loss is unthinkable. Such buildings certainly deserve to be defended as objects in their own right. They should be sorted out from the rest, protected and preserved for their singularity. They may be monuments more than "Landmarks," since their present situation is often irrelevant, but it is a worthy and urgent part of any city's responsibility to preserve them. Preservationism must be a component of protecting a city's essential form.

An equally fundamental aspect of protection can be distinguished as *conservationism*. If this principle is firmly established and operating smoothly, there is no need for emergency rescue, indignant editorials, or financial support. It can be accomplished by nurturing rather than trying to reimpose urban continuity.

Conservationism

If cast-iron Worth Street (see page 164) had continued to be the partial home of the textile industry, for example — if the industry had been encouraged to remain in that area, with zoning favoring the trade and fire regulations coaxing improvement of the property rather than abandonment of it — then perhaps that would have been enough to keep the industry from moving uptown. Demand for new commercial space might have been directed against ramshackle real estate in the vicinity, and Worth Street, the historic center, could have been designated for preservation if necessary. The chances are that legal preservation would then have been only a safeguard, and not a necessity.

Worth Street was architecturally meritorious when the buildings were used merely as lofts. Rehabilitated as corporate offices, the street would have been one of the greatest ensembles in America — and would have presented an aspect that the invisible images of "Madison Avenue," "Wall Street," and, sadly, "Seventh Avenue" lack entirely. When most of Worth Street was demolished for a parking lot a few years ago, timely preservation legislation could have saved it. But the infinitely more complex and finally more gratifying measures of urban conservation should have been used to begin with.

The ideal way of establishing a sense of continuity in cities combines both preservation and conservation — different but compatible techniques. One of the tasks of municipal government should be to promote thrift through the conservation of urban form. This can be done with the intelligent exercise of existing government powers.

And why not urban conservation? We recognize the need to conserve every other aspect and resource of our environment. Ultimately, a stand of Douglas Fir or Redwood is more easily replaceable than the forms that evoke a bit of human history. Conservation is not necessarily an act practiced by conservatives. It is concerned with the search for best use as well as thrift. It calls for active perception and timely and imaginative decisions if anything is to pay off. If the best use is to be made of urban resources, there has to be endless vigilance by city planners. It is, in a way, the opposite of preservationism, where a law is passed in a moment and then the constant job of holding back change begins. In urban conservation, the work to use things to best advantage is continuous. Only the rewards are simple and self-accomplished.

What needs to be sought and conserved are the basic things in the city, the truthful things measured by human experience, though not necessarily those most clear and well-ordered and visual. These should be things that state the case of the city from its birth — things which, in summary, have been called here the city's "essential form." The solution to the problem of survival should begin with an analysis of what that essential form is, and the public must participate in the discussion.

A conservation program can then be performed by elected officials and planners. They need to be as circumspect in the prevention of waste as careful naturalists or ecologists, and as considerate of life. They need to be preoccupied with the entire system, history and structure of the city — and seek not only to improve its operations and extend its possibilities, but to conserve its natural and unnatural resources. They not only must be able to change the form of the city, they must also defend it — by practicing *conservation of form.* The second is the more difficult job.

In New York, Le Corbusier believed, change was the fixed condition. Its basic nature, character, steady state was change; what got saved and preserved was a radical variable. New York to him was "A city which will be replaced by another city." It is very likely indeed that change is one of the fundamental New York characteristics. It was one of the great, disturbing symbols of Herzog's world in Saul Bellow's novel. Moses Herzog is forever passing scenes of demolition. Park Avenue is filled with construction machinery and smells of cement. The city is summed up by a series of taxi rides and walks through dust:

At the corner he paused to watch the work of the wrecking crew. The great metal ball swung at the walls, passed easily through brick, and entered the rooms, the lazy weight browsing on kitchens and parlors. Everything it touched wavered and burst, spilled down. There rose a white tranquil cloud of plaster dust. The afternoon was ending, and in the widening area of demolition was a fire, fed by the wreckage. Moses heard the air, softly pulled toward the flames, felt the heat. The workmen, heaping the bonfire with wood, threw strips of moulding like javelins. Paint and varnish smoked like incense. The old flooring burned gratefully — the funeral of exhausted objects. Scaffolds walled with pink, white, green doors quivered as the six-wheeled trucks carried off fallen brick. The sun, now leaving for New Jersey and the west, was surrounded by a dazzling broth of atmospheric gases. Herzog observed that people were spattered with red stains, and that he himself was flecked on the arms and chest. He crossed Seventh Avenue and entered the subway.*

If perpetual change is the destiny of New York, it might not have to be at the cost of such devastation and bloodletting. Believing it to be the price of progress, New Yorkers are remarkably cheerful about destruction. They have faith that their city is in the process of adapting itself better to their needs, even if the reverse may be true.

Perpetual change is just as difficult to live with as perpetual unchange. The city of Venice faces the other problem. The entire city is treated as a museum, and since there is no intention of materially altering it, the lives of its citizens must be adapted to whatever can be made of the old city form — mostly tourism

---

* Saul Bellow, *Herzog*, Viking Press, 1964.

and old crafts, with essential services. They are committed everlastingly to the same urban order of things that served well centuries before. The frozen past is undoubtedly a curse and hardship for many. Yet should the world be deprived of Venice? Should Italy? Should those of its inhabitants who love it? Perhaps the question of change in both New York and Venice is resolved by the fact that a city ultimately selects its own people. Those who live in Venice do so partly because it is unlike anyplace else.

Most New Yorkers who have been chosen by their city are prepared to accept economic imperatives as sufficient reason for change. Fortunately, the economics of building are the easiest to manipulate in order to favor beneficial change. Government is already doing it with taxes and laws and regulations. But it is still considered a rather radical idea to expect these uncoordinated powers to help carry out planning policy instead of, as frequently happens, obstructing it.*

Future change

In New York's early planning, the form of the city was established as a linear development, moving north from the tip of Manhattan Island. That this was indeed fundamental and prophetic was demonstrated by the fact that through *laissez-faire* action alone, the center of gravity of the city moved uptown to 23rd Street, 34th Street, 59th Street. There it stopped, and later growth has been mostly accompanied by self-destruction. But here lies a useful principle. If postwar planning had been concerned with urban conservation, it might have been possible to direct the explosive expansion of management facilities up to Central Park North or perhaps Fordham Road in the Bronx, instead of letting it destroy part of Park Avenue. Indeed, the expansion might have moved any place in the city, north or south, which was weak in form but well situated and well connected with transportation.

Public transit, present or contemplated, might be providing the matrix for change. Year by year, a complex of new facilities for the movement of people and goods should be carried forward as part of a development plan. When new intersections on the transit matrix have been established, both public improvement and heavy incentives to private investment should follow. New York has miles and miles of nebulous suburbs to spare. The time and effort of building should be directed towards making them identifiable city sub-centers, instead of eradicating the existing city.

New York, as well as other cities, can fulfill its destiny through changing its weakest elements. These are the things that are unessential in terms of the present or the past. The evolving form of the city ought to be an affirmation of the relevance of life to the uniqueness of the place.

Technology has recently provided us with revolutionary opportunities for change. Anything can be built, moved, or destroyed. Now is the last possible moment for resisting the acts of destruction that would separate us finally from earlier experience. For unlike history, unlike politics or philosophy or even art, the environment allows the actual experience of cultural continuity to be felt — an experience to be cherished by children as much as (or perhaps more than) by savants and scholars.

---

* As an example, there is no reason for real estate taxes to be uniform. They might be zoned by a planning body to correspond with development needs, perhaps with a ten-year lag to permit adjustment, and as a precaution against improper use of the power.

20

Ultimately, the need for change, like anything else in building, ought to be determined by the needs of the users. Where the city form is concerned, not only are the owners of a particular property the users but also everyone who passes and sees it. Existing places are truly *time-honored*. Strictly speaking, everything is time-honored and ought to be considered as such when change is contemplated. But of all things, certainly architecture has aspects most concerned with time. Architecture provides the only measurable way to discover the past in the urban environment, and its conservation is therefore not only expedient but vital. A city can be complete and unique only in relation to its own history and essential form, and this must be reawakened, discovered anew, or sought and defended.

THE URBAN SCENE AND PUBLIC PLACES.

The Greek agora, the medieval marketplace, and the Italian piazza served their cities by providing convenient places where human interaction naturally occurred. These squares originated in the need for public assembly, and were situated in the principal centers of activity. New York's natural meeting places are far less formal. With the city's regular blocks and relatively wide sidewalks, paths and purposes can interact along the street (on front steps, around pushcarts, on avenues during a lunch hour); in the neighborhood parks and playgrounds (particularly at the promenades lined with benches that are adjacent to buildings); or at railroad stations, airports, even at taxi stands outside hotels. These are all public places in the sense that they provide for interaction and encounter. It is characteristic of New York that an informal public nexus is usually a point along a route, a place to pause before moving on to the next destination.

Like most American cities, New York would benefit from having more places planned for casual public encounter. But once it becomes clear that public places need not be narrowly defined as primarily architectural or monumental in character, measures can be taken to conserve the vitality of those we now have. Vitality can be eroded. A conservation program should guard against even the seemingly trivial changes in urban operations that reduce the richness of use. For example, making city avenues one-way discourages the casual stroller because of the intrusion of faster and noisier vehicular traffic. The same act moves bus routes to alternate avenues, often 1600 feet apart, thus halving the opportunity of access to buses. Yet multiple opportunities are exactly what city streets need to remain vital.

Some parts of New York's urban scene are famous throughout the world. The skyline and downtown canyons of the financial district are magnificent because they are vivid, practical and unique. They are a clear representation of commercial enterprise, valuable land, and the necessity of good communications. It is significant that they grew up in a direct self-determined way, before limitations were set on the bulk and height of buildings. As a testament to the essential formation of New York, this part of the urban scene provides us with some straightforward truth about the city.

"Space in the image of man is *place*," says the architect Aldo van Eyck. Public places are created by human use, not the other way around. Clear urban configurations reveal significant characteristics of human use adapted to the place. Usually those characteristics which most clearly depict essential aspects of the city are those best loved. They throb with life created by history, but seem quite free of time.

The Grand Army Plaza, or as it is usually called, the Plaza — the widening of Fifth Avenue before Central Park. The Plaza Hotel (right), an earlier namesake of the present building on the same spot, was begun in 1881 by the firm of Fife and Campbell, but was held up for eight years by litigation. It opened in 1890, but then closed in 1905, to be demolished and replaced by architect Henry J. Hardenbergh's Plaza two years later. The Plaza fountain, designed by Thomas Hastings and topped with Karl Bitter's statue of "Abundance," was not built until 1916 upon Joseph Pulitzer's $50,000 bequest.

1   2

THE PLAZA'S PLAZA.   Most of the great European squares are spaces defined by their walls; that is to say, it is enclosure that matters. The character of the square is distinguished mainly by the architecture surrounding it, and buildings give the open space its scale and form. However, in New York's Plaza almost all the buildings which form the surrounding walls have been replaced one or more times. The Hotel Netherland (1, right), north of 59th Street, was supplanted by the Sherry-Netherland. Leading to the square, "Marble Row," an elegant street of individual town houses (see pages 26 and 124) which ran between 57th and 58th Streets on the east side of Fifth Avenue (2, left), is now gone. Most splendid of all the Plaza's vanished buildings was Cornelius Vanderbilt's mansion, directly to the south (3, and see pages 111 and 121).

Some of the earlier buildings which are "lost" here were fortunately not elements fundamental to the Plaza as an urban space. The secret of the Plaza, and its character and importance, really lies not in buildings but in the New York grid of streets which is so seldom interrupted by anything, especially by a green space. Here at last Fifth Avenue breaks loose from two walls and, at 58th Street, opens wide into a three-sided square before it gets to the vaster freedom of Central Park a block to the north. The generator of this singular urban space is the traffic system. Only the Plaza Hotel, by accident the longest-lasting element on the scene, functions in architectural terms. Though the hotel was named for the square, the square now seems a forecourt for the hotel, and the building becomes a pivot-point at two crucial streets.

What remains essential — given the Plaza's almost unique urban basis — is the preservation of force of the street lines. However, on the site of the Savoy-Plaza Hotel (4, left), a new office building is being built which is set back from the straight wall of buildings along Fifth Avenue, and this notch in the wall will fracture the characteristic system of the square.

24

3

4

TRIUMPHAL ARCHES.   The temporary wooden arch that Stanford White designed in 1889 for the centennial of George Washington's inauguration (1) proved a suitable terminus for Fifth Avenue at a time when the houses adjacent to Washington Square were low enough to stand modestly beside it (see page 42).   White's later masonry arch is now permanently in place — not spanning the Avenue, but back into the Square.   In 1892, the 400th anniversary of Columbus Day was celebrated with the temporary erection of a triumphal arch at Fifth Avenue and 57th Street (2 — Marble Row is at the right of the north-facing view).   The plaster and wood arch built for the return of Admiral Dewey in 1899 (3) was a collaboration by G. R. Lamb, architect, with members of the National Sculpture Society. Fifth Avenue and 23rd Street was the site, and it was still important enough as a city nexus twenty years later to be chosen as the location for another parade structure, an Arch of Victory for the American Expeditionary Force.

Temporary festival structures are works which are generally associated with the late Renaissance and Baroque.   Yet the idea of building a decorative arch, rather than a mere reviewing stand, still seems appropriate for public ceremonies — and the way the 23rd Street arches defined an amorphous street intersection indicated something that was even worth making permanent.

1   2   3

1   2

EARLY GRAND CENTRAL TERMINALS.   The first Grand Central (1) was built in 1871 for the New York and Harlem, New York and New Haven, and New York Central Railroads. The rugged mansard-roofed wings flanking a central block formed an outline imitated by the Grand Union Hotel, from which this photo was taken. The depot was enlarged in 1899, and redesigned by C. P. R. Gilbert according to the stylistic modes of its own decade (2). The acquisition of underground track rights in 1903 made the present terminal necessary.

1

THE GRAND CENTRAL SKYLINE.   The railroad tracks buried under Park Avenue established a new visual configuration for the avenue and for the buildings on it. The New York Central office building, its odd Gothic-style corbelled tower ending the vista, came to characterize Park Avenue (1), and appropriately so. With its outline and decoration, it was able to indicate clearly its relationship to the height of a man, and so was able to convey to the observer its own true size. It therefore was like an enormous measuring-rod, and from miles off along Park Avenue the dimensions of half a city could be

3

perceived with its help. This visual indicator, which explained scale so simply, was lost when the new Pan Am building obliterated the Park Avenue skyline with its own undifferentiated silhouette.

Scale and clarity are likewise fortified when important interior spaces are revealed as impressive volumes in the urban scene. The Grand Central Waiting Room and Concourse was a clear form which was coherently scaled when other buildings deferred to it (3), before the Pan Am building was built. Almost four blocks of distance could be judged between the sculptured entablature of the Terminal and the lanterned roof of the New York Central Building (4). And Warren & Wetmore's auto ramps, which carry Park Avenue on a breathtaking ride around Grand Central, were much more potent when there was more sky to be seen among the buildings (2).

2

4

PENNSYLVANIA STATION.   Work began on Penn Station in 1906, following the designs of McKim, Mead and White, with Charles Follen McKim as Partner-in-Charge. According to contemporary accounts, the "great quarry" made by the excavation was comparable to the building of the Panama Canal. The design was also a conscious enough attempt on the part of the Pennsylvania Railroad Company to establish the importance of railroads by building a pre-eminent building, a civic masterpiece. What the newspapers called an "undertaking without precedent" was therefore fairly considered to have exceeded the greatest public efforts of history.

When it was completed in 1910, New York had a station built with the grandeur of Rome (in fact, it was supposed to be a replica of the Caracalla Baths). But behind the ingenuous magniloquence of its facades (1) was the genuine majesty of its steel-ribbed spaces (7). The great Train Concourse was covered with acres of glass in domes, arches and vaults (2) — a free translation of masonry forms into the fragile elements of machine technology; and not so much in the academic tradition of historicism as in the new tradition of the Crystal Palaces and the glass galleries and halls of Paris exhibitions. This was the space the spectator saw as he arrived in New York: the corrugated glass roof arches and domes (3) and the main Concourse an open level above the tracks (4).

2

From there, before the addition of the tawdry new ticket office which closed the passage, the arriving
visitor moved past the lesser waiting rooms into the General Waiting Room. He was confronted by an
enormous vaulted space (5), this time done more conventionally with coffered plasterwork hung from
the concealed steel structure. Telephones, parcel and ticket offices were located in this hall. A Lunch
Room and more formal Dining Room (see page 56) lay beyond, flanking the grand staircase on the procession east — then along a lofty arcade to the vestibule and the street at Seventh Avenue. Alternatively,
if the visitor had baggage and wanted a taxi, he could emerge directly from the General Waiting Room
into a carriageway on either the north or south side of the station (6).

3

4

5

6

Mass Assembly and Mass Movement were clearly defined by the station, but it had also an undoubted nobility which it imparted to the observer — "Or did," commented Lewis Mumford, "until that structure was converted by its thoughtful guardians into a vast jukebox . . ." And yet it remained — a majestic threshold into the headquarters city for the traveler from Glen Cove or Chicago. It seemed as if it would take a new Flood to sweep it away.

"Until the first blow fell," the *New York Times* wrote on October 30, 1963, "no one was convinced that Penn Station really would be demolished or that New York would permit this monumental act of vandalism . . . Any city gets what it admires, will pay for, and ultimately deserves. Even when we had Penn Station, we couldn't afford to keep it clean. We want and deserve tin-can architecture in a tin-horn

7

8

9

culture. And we will probably be judged not by the monuments we build but by those we have destroyed."
The station was sacrificed through application of the real-estate logic that often dictates the demolition
of the very building that makes an area desirable (8, 9). In a letter to the *Times*, the President of the
Pennsylvania Railroad Company asked, "Does it make any sense to preserve a building merely as a
'monument'?"

1

CENTRAL PARK AS PLANNED.   In 1851, there was nothing that could be called a park in America. For a natural public place, New York had the parade ground at the Battery. The first suggestions for a large city park came from William Cullen Bryant, a town dweller who missed his rural pleasures, and from Andrew J. Downing, a landscape architect impressed with the parks of Europe. Mayor Kingsland became interested, and in 1853 the principle was approved by the New York Board of Aldermen. A competition was held in 1858, won by Frederick Law Olmsted and Calvert Vaux. By this time the site had been changed from a forested area along the East River to a rather barren tract in the center of the island, chiefly because it could be obtained at lower cost.

The sparseness of natural riches provided Olmsted and Vaux with the opportunity to design a park according to the precepts of English landscape gardening. One of the lessons taught by the British work of William Kent, Capability Brown, and Humphry Repton was that the creation of perfect natural landscape was essentially an artistic and artificial effort: a garden should be an earthly paradise, an Eden, a representation of nature in well-balanced perfection. Central Park's bare tract therefore was designed

2

3

to epitomize and condense the greatest possible variety of woods and water, tangles, cascades, and craggy heights. After the park had been built according to this plan and had been growing for forty years, a New York historian proudly directed attention to "the craft of the illusion and the perfection of the art that can produce such a panorama of Nature in so little space" (E. I. Zeisloft, *The New Metropolis*, 1899).

Olmsted's 800-acre landscape design depended on contrasts between wild and tamed parts, open vistas and densely planted sections. The dense planting (1, 3) began to be removed when New York police operations suggested the elimination of shrubbery that might conceal anybody. Appropriate park structures by Vaux and others — such as a bandstand (2) — have vanished, and the park has instead become a building site for dozens of anti-garden philanthropic monuments, from skating rinks and theaters to a grotesque "Children's Zoo."

One hears that the park is dangerous, and this becomes a self-fulfilling prophecy as fewer and fewer go there, maintenance decreases, amenities vanish. Central Park, once a model of the perfection of nature, now seems to be an official maintenance problem — a natural one, like six inches of snow. Disposal is the treatment it has been receiving.

41

SCALE OF BUILDINGS TO STREETS.　　Fifth Avenue from the top of Washington Arch (1), until quite recently, was virtually the same quiet residential street that Henry James knew, even though familiar landmarks were vanishing. Soon after the period of his *Washington Square*, the Brevoort House was demolished (see page 117), and the Brevoort Hotel (the white building on the right-hand side of the street) began its slow decline before it met its dusty death. But when tall apartment houses were built on lower Fifth Avenue a few years ago, the new buildings finally shattered the relationship of building height to street width that was the street's essential characteristic. This has permanently

1

altered the walk up scale and obviously residential character of a famous milieu.

A very different scale had been established on Park Avenue, where the great street width was made necessary by the underground New York Central tracks (2). Real park malls once ran down the center of Park Avenue's midtown area, bringing the width down to human size, and in scale with the existing residential buildings. The park malls were destroyed in 1927 when they were reduced to narrow traffic islands, in order to give motor vehicles more room. Almost all the buildings shown here have been replaced by office blocks, including the Sheraton East Hotel (right, beyond St. Bartholomew's Church).

2

PRIVATE GATHERING PLACES.

Against William Penn's "The public must and will be served" can be set William H. Vanderbilt's "The public be damned!" as a remark perhaps more characteristic of New York. The public is actually served and damned in different ways, often for profit. Privately run accommodations are as socially essential as public places. They enclose important public activities such as political meetings, dining, playgoing, and in the past, even gambling. The only thing really "private" about a hotel or a meeting hall is its ownership.

Stanford White's Madison Square Garden, one of the most popular, useful, and worthwhile of buildings, provides a reasonable example. It was sold because the operators thought a cheaper building would be better able to pay its way, and since the site was in demand, cash was available. Under the circumstances complete financing was readily found for a new building, the old one was sold, and the new one went up. Based in part on the proceeds of the old building's sale, the new Garden was expected to show a satisfactory profit — a familiar story in real estate. But was it ever considered that the first building was better than the one that replaced it? Or that the original location adjacent to Madison Square Park was much more desirable, for the city's sake? If these matters had been responsibly taken into account, the outcome undoubtedly would have been different. Maintenance of worthwhile private gathering places is strongly in the public interest and should therefore be made attractive to owners by the city. But the basic responsibility for maintaining private property is a private one.

In changing aspects of cities there is a certain point where public interests can be completely neglected, and private operators allowed to dispose of their property as they wish. This point ought to be clearly defined as the place where all public access stops. Certainly the privilege of running a place of public accommodation for profit bears with it certain civic responsibilities. A private owner should be prepared to accept the legal necessity for practicing conservation on his own premises when the services he offers — including also the building that he has provided — turn out to be essential public commodities.

The 26th floor tower lounge of The Panhellenic, designed by John Mead Howells, was built in 1928 at First Avenue and 49th Street and subsequently called the Beekman Tower Hotel. The building has now been converted into apartments.

BROADWAY TABERNACLE. The Broadway Tabernacle stood at 340 to 344 Broadway, between Worth Street and Catherine Lane. It was built by a church society in 1836 to promote the growth of New England Congregationalism in New York, but its most memorable function was its service for a while as the city's main meeting hall. Many anti-slavery rallies were held at the Tabernacle, and numerous old prints show how frequently the hall was the scene of important public events. The view here is of the ratification meeting of Millard Fillmore as candidate of the American Party in 1856.

The Tabernacle was sold and demolished in 1857 to make way for a dry goods warehouse. Funds from the sale were used to build a neo-Gothic Congregational church at Sixth Avenue and 34th Street.

46

NIBLO'S GARDEN.   Nine blocks uptown from the Tabernacle was Niblo's Garden and Theater, at Broadway and Prince Street. It was built in 1827 and was first known as the Sans Souci. For a while the Garden was the major New York exhibition hall, hired out for various displays and fairs. This watercolor shows the annual exhibit (about 1845) of the American Institute, an organization which promoted advancement in commerce, agriculture and the arts.

The Garden and Theater was twice rebuilt after fires in 1846 and 1872. Theater fires caused fearful losses in New York — King's 1893 *Handbook of New York City* records thirty-seven theaters burned during the preceding century. Stringent building laws aimed at providing for fire protection in places of public assembly were finally passed in 1887.

THE GERMAN WINTER GARDEN.   Many private gathering places in New York offered special amusement in the foreign traditions of some of the city's residents. Partly to circumvent Sunday blue laws, a number of German beer gardens were established where Sabbath "Sacred Concerts" were held, and beer, radishes, cheese and Strauss waltzes could be enjoyed after payment of a small admission fee. The police apparently overlooked these early speakeasies, which were — behind plain facades — some of New York's most charming and elaborate meeting rooms. This watercolor shows the German Winter Garden which once stood at 45 Bowery. It was built around 1855, and the dome was one of the earliest made with cast-iron rib framing.

ATLANTIC GARDEN.   Another celebrated German beer hall was Atlantic Garden, at 50 Bowery, between Bayard and Canal Streets, across the street from the German Winter Garden and just north of the Thalia Theater (see page 76). This engraving from *Harper's Magazine* shows the festivities on the occasion of the capitulation of Sedan to Germany, September 10, 1870. By this time, the most prominent German gathering place, Terrace Garden, had been established on 58th Street near Lexington Avenue. It had followed the German population over toward Yorkville, as the Bowery area was becoming run down. Terrace Garden was demolished in 1927. The last available view of the vanished Atlantic Garden is a 1922 photo owned by the New-York Historical Society, which shows this room to have turned dingy, though still as imposing as it seems below.

1

THE GARDEN AT MADISON SQUARE.   The site of the first Madison Square
Garden was an entire block bounded by Madison and Fourth Avenues and 26th and 27th Streets. In
1873 it held a performing arena adapted from railroad sheds which P. T. Barnum leased from Commodore
Vanderbilt (1, center). It was originally known as the Great Roman Hippodrome, then as Gilmore's
Garden (after the new leaseholder), and finally as Madison Square Garden when William H. Vanderbilt
repossessed it in 1879. Pugilism, legal for the first time in New York, was the Garden's lucrative mainstay.
The arena was in one of the city's most fashionable areas; it was across the park from the Fifth Avenue

2

Hotel (see page 71), and just north of the former Leonard Jerome mansion (1 and 2, right — the balconies are now gone but the building has become a designated Landmark).

The National Horse Show Association, formed in 1883, secured the property with the aid of J. P. Morgan. On the site they planned an elegant new home for the annual horse show, and held an architectural competition which was won by McKim, Mead and White. Stanford White became deeply engrossed in the project. He successfully argued for the completion of all aspects of his design, including a theater, a restaurant, a concert hall, a roof garden, a tower to be the second highest structure in the city, and arcades

which covered the sidewalks so the building would seem even closer to Madison Square Park. It was constructed as White had hoped (2) — of yellow brick and Pompeian white terra cotta, with an interior painted pink with cream-colored iron arched trusses (3). Augustus Saint-Gaudens provided a nude statute of Diana to top the spire, which became famous in its own right.

On June 16, 1890, the Garden opened its doors to 17,000 people, and as the contemporary press noted, it joined the Metropolitan Opera House and Carnegie Hall as one of the city's principal places of amusement. In magnitude, the Garden was the most important of the three. White took personal responsibility for its beauty, its critical success, and, ultimately, the blame for its financial failure. The Garden absorbed him even after completion. For the Columbian Quatercentenary in 1892 he made New York streets a carnival of lights with Edison's new incandescent bulbs, and Madison Square Garden, its tower spectacularly lit at night, was a big part of the show (4).

White was shot to death in the roof garden in 1906 by a deranged Pittsburgh millionaire, and in the succeeding years his beloved Garden succumbed to foreclosure by the New York Life Insurance Company. It was at last demolished in 1925, the final lessee making no attempt to save it, though he managed to raise six million dollars for the construction of a new Garden away from Madison Square.

TAMMANY HALL.   The New York Tammany Society was founded in 1789, growing out of the earlier Sons of Liberty.   Like other Tammany organizations in other states it was named after Tamanend, Indian chief of the Delawares, and many of its observances and titles were borrowed from the Indians.   In New York Aaron Burr was instrumental in setting up Tammany as a political power. The tiger, its famous symbol, was contributed by Mayor "Boss" Tweed.

The Society had four Wigwams in its history.   Its famous second home was on Park Row and Frankfort Street, which was taken over by *The Sun* when Tammany moved to a new building in 1868.   This one went up on the north side of 14th Street, between Third Avenue and Irving Place (2), next to the original Academy of Music (see page 79).   Tony Pastor's Theater, a small variety house, operated within Tammany Hall from about 1877.

1

54

2

A color lithograph of the main hall shows an "Interior View of Tammany Hall Decorated for the National Convention, July 4th 1888" (1). This splendid room was demolished, along with the rest of the block, to make way for Consolidated Edison's office building. A new Tammany Hall was built on 17th Street and Fourth Avenue in 1929, but it is now a trade union hall. Tammany had long since become a euphemism for political bossism, and the "Society of Tammany or Columbian Order," which showed immigrants how to vote, elected Negro Aldermen, and organized candidates for Labor, today survives only in name.

1

RESTAURANTS.   Since restaurants usually occupy rented quarters, they are frequently the most short-lived of those private gathering places open to the public. Their impermanence may be due as often to gastronomic decline as to expiring leases. Architecturally, few can afford to create a complete milieu — it can only be a case of a new shop interior which changes scenery from the pharmacy that may have been there before, as a shoe repair shop might change it again later on. One such example was the vanished Broadmoor Restaurant, in a building on East 41st Street. Its interior (1) was designed by Ely Jacques Kahn. The decoration, characteristic of the '30s, appears to have been appropriately easy to paint over.

2

4

5

Some of the few New York restaurants actually run in homes of their own were among the most beloved and memorable. The Dining Room at Pennsylvania Station (2) was in a magnificent hall designed for it, and the Claremont Inn (3), converted from a country house before the Civil War, was a popular objective for excursions. The Inn was on Riverside Drive just north of Grant's Tomb until it was burned and demolished by the city in 1951.

Probably the most famous New York restaurant was Delmonico's. It started on William Street in the 1820s, and after nine moves arrived at the northeast corner of Fifth Avenue and 44th Street, in a building designed by James Brown Lord (4). The wrought-iron covered doors were opened in 1897, and closed forever in 1923 when the many dining rooms, ballrooms, supper-rooms and "bachelor apartments" were slated for destruction. Sherry's, Delmonico's great rival, had closed four years earlier for similar reasons, a victim — as Louis Sherry put it — of "Prohibition and war-born Bolshevism."

While it was a little harder to work out what could be done about Bolshevism, the end of Prohibition saw the old Central Park Casino glorified by Joseph Urban. The Black and Gold Room (5) was one of the rooms he redecorated in 1933, only a few years before the city tore down the entire building.

New York dining and drinking places have often had their own special design language, including the familiar covered-wagon canopy (6), and the long mahogany bar. The canopies remain, if not at the Crillon on 48th Street then at a thousand other restaurants all over the city; but many of the old zinc-and-mahogany-and-cut-glass taverns that once lined Sixth Avenue and Third Avenue have been altered beyond recognition, or have vanished for good.

CANFIELD'S GAMBLING HOUSE.   Richard Canfield, who had been a nightclerk in a Union Square hotel in the 1870s, later moved uptown to become proprietor of his own gaming establishment at 5 East 44th Street. Canfield's Gambling House was infamously attractive to society layabouts. On one night in 1902, Reginald Claypoole Vanderbilt — still an undergraduate at Yale — reportedly dropped $70,000 at a session in one of the gaming rooms, perhaps this one.

Canfield's was the only prominent New York example of the casino life legally accessible in Europe, and there were many who loved the place. The imposing interiors survived until the late 1920s when the site was taken over for an office building.

HOTELS.   Many prominent New York hotels had disappeared even before the old Waldorf-Astoria was built. In Revolutionary times there were Bunker's, the Washington Tavern, Burn's and the Tontine Coffee Houses. In the 19th century, among the famous hotels which vanished were the St. Nicholas, Metropolitan, New York, Victoria, St. James, and the Brunswick on Fifth Avenue. Unlike most real estate redevelopment, these early hotels were frequently victims of actual obsolescence. Once prime lodgings, they gave way to a new standard of accommodation.

Hotels were originally inns which attempted only to provide satisfactory food and comfortable shelter for travelers. But starting with the construction of the Brunswick, luxury and elegance began to be made

1   3

part of New York hotels as well. Because enough people could afford it and because fashionable New York society was making its own rules, the hotels started to purvey not only extremely comfortable quarters, but also undisputed social dignity. The new New York hotels were built to be homes for the quality, while elegant European hotels of the same period were still the rather disreputable transient places of Feydeau farces. Prosperous New Yorkers found that they did not need to maintain town residences if social standing was equally assured at certain hotels. To make way for this assurance, hotels that could not be transformed from mere public inns either went into decline or were discarded. The new hotels, besides providing such modern comforts as central heating, also offered shops and galleries, ballrooms, Royal Suites, and lecture halls. It became more common to take meals at a hotel under that lately rediscovered idea called the American Plan. In his 1899 book *The New Metropolis*, E. I. Zeisloft found that "People come to these colossal buildings, cities in themselves, not only for short stays, but for months at a time."

The Waldorf-Astoria was the most famous hotel to meet these transformed standards. The Waldorf part (3, left) was built in 1893 by William Waldorf Astor; then the rest of it, the Astoria (3, center and right), was added in 1895–97 by his aunt. Henry J. Hardenbergh was the architect. Dozens of the rooms and halls were at the disposal of the general public, including the Turkish Salon (1), where coffee was served by a genuine Turk and a boy assistant. Some were accessible by such grand galleries as Peacock Alley (2). Zeisloft marveled that "The poorest man living in or visiting New York, provided he is well dressed, may sit about these corridors night after night, spending never a cent, speaking to no one, and he will be allowed to stay."

The old Waldorf-Astoria met its end in a typical New York way: since the entire block was already under one ownership, it was cheaper for the builders of the future Empire State Building to buy it than to try to acquire nearby property piecemeal. One of the city's most valuable buildings consequently was demolished in 1929.

5

Splendor and elegance were characteristic not only of Manhattan hotels. Brooklyn had two on Coney Island, when that part of Brooklyn was still a long day's trip away from downtown New York. One of them was the Oriental, and the other the Manhattan Beach Hotel (4). The Manhattan Beach was really a resort hotel, only open during the summer season. Its electrically illuminated advertising sign at 23rd Street and Broadway, "Swept

7

by Ocean Breezes," was for a while a great New York curiosity. The Grand View Hotel (5), which once stood in the Fort Hamilton section of Brooklyn, was undoubtedly a less luxurious place, despite its splendid ornamented galleries. The grand view referred to was presumably the Narrows and the Lower Bay.

As the Grand View was built in a timber style characteristic of its probable construction date in the '70s, the Park Avenue Hotel by John Kellum (6), on 33rd Street in Manhattan, was a typical masonry building of the same decade. Originally established in 1878 as a home for working women by the merchant prince A. T. Stewart, it became a luxury hotel when strict house rules made the first scheme a failure. It was torn down in 1927. The Murray Hill Hotel (7), nearby at Park Avenue between 40th and 41st Streets, was a seven-story building with two pointed corner towers and over 500 rooms. Its site now holds an office building.

8

The beginning of the fashion for living in the country and boarding in town probably began with the opening of the Astor House (8) in 1836, designed by Isaiah Rogers and sensational for its interior plumbing on all floors. It stood on Broadway between Vesey and Barclay Streets, a square building with a square courtyard inside until part of it was demolished in 1913, the rest following in 1926. Meanwhile the fashionable hotel district had long since shifted from lower Broadway. For a while it centered on the Madison Square area, where the Fifth Avenue Hotel stood (9) on Fifth Avenue between 23rd and 24th Streets, built 1856–58 with the first New York hotel elevator by William Washburn, architect. During the Columbian Quatercentenary, *The Times* of London said that no hostelry in the world had ever entertained so many distinguished people. It was demolished in 1908, only sixteen years later, for by

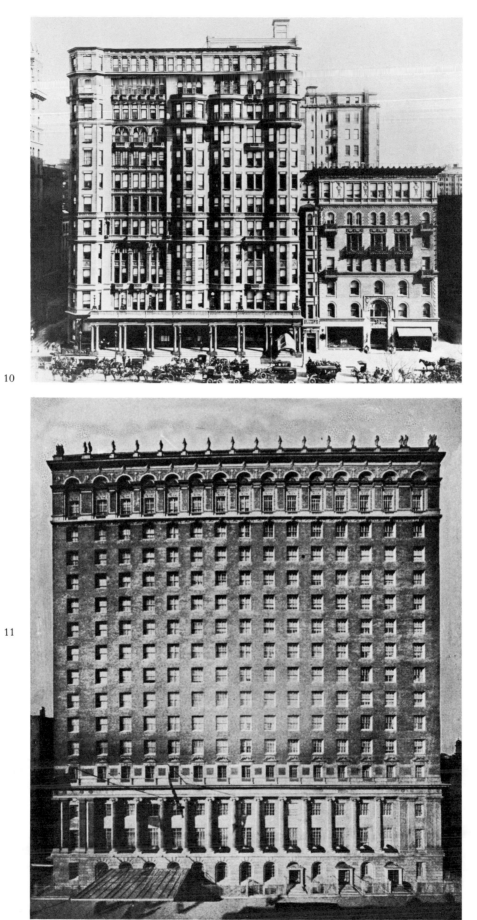

9

10

11

12   13

14

then the best neighborhoods — and best hotels — were far uptown. One of these was the Savoy (10), on the east side of the Plaza at 59th Street, built in 1890–92 after designs by Ralph S. Townsend. This hotel and the Bolkenhayn Apartments next to it were torn down in 1926 to make way for the grander Savoy-Plaza Hotel (see page 25).

There are those who believe that the finest of·all New York hotels was the Ritz-Carlton (11), by Warren & Wetmore, architects of the new Grand Central Terminal. The Ritz-Carlton, on Madison Avenue and 46th Street, reached its fashionable heyday at about the time of the First World War. Its ballrooms and lobbies (12, 13), and some say its service and general *ambiance*, were better than those furnished later elsewhere at the Ritz Tower. The Ritz-Carlton was razed in 1951 to provide a site for an office building.

Hotels were often engulfed by the prosperity they created. The Buckingham (14), on Fifth Avenue between 49th and 50th Streets, found itself a perfect location when it was built in the 1870s, and the fashionable district moved up around it. But ultimately the site proved too perfect, since it became valuable enough to be bought up for the construction of a department store.

New York hotel building now appears to have gone through two complete cycles — first the era of comfortable city inns, typified by the Brevoort and the old Fifth Avenue hotels; then the period of luxurious elegance of which the old Waldorf-Astoria and the Ritz-Carlton were examples. The hotels of the second cycle, by setting a new standard, did much to undermine the prosperity of the first. A third cycle of New York hotel building has now begun, based on the idea of standardized mass accommodation. However, the tourist and convention trade currently being sought is not the same as the clientele still being provided for by the remaining accommodations of the second cycle. It would be sad for New York if the newest hotels were permitted to eradicate the last of the luxury palaces.

1

THEATERS.   Of all the institutions associated with civic advance, theaters have probably been the most highly esteemed. From the mid-18th century, when theaters were instruments for the enhancement of society and fashion, to the mid-20th century, when they are supposed to be vessels of culture, new theaters have been credited as being the fairest architectural examples of the splendor and spirit of the community. Even privately-owned theaters, operated for profit, have been hailed as municipal improvements when built, when in fact — as has frequently occurred in New York — they may have supplanted better buildings. Change has often been more characteristic than improvement, though fire was frequently to blame. The rapid rate of new theater building in New York has far outstripped advancements in theater technology. It would seem that new theaters, like a woman's annual spring fashions, are primarily meant to support ideas of freshness, reaffirmation and vitality. This being so, it is no wonder that the old gowns are pushed to the back of the closet.

3

A few wholly modern New York theaters have already vanished. The Center Theater in Rockefeller Center (1, 2), built as recently as 1932 by the architects Reinhard & Hofmeister, Corbett Harrison & MacMurray, and Hood & Fouilhoux, had an auditorium (2) quite as good if somewhat less stunning than their nearby Radio City Music Hall. And some of the interior design, such as Edward Steichen's photo mural in the Men's Smoking Room (1), far surpassed any of the callow artwork which survives at Rockefeller Center. But the Center Theater has now been renovated out of existence — filled in with levels of office floors — because its theatrical uses, even for television work, were not as profitable as its potential use as offices.

There is some doubt about the date of the earliest theatrical performance in New York City. Probably there was no such thing under the Dutch. The first record of the appearance of a professional actor was in 1730, during the British colonial administration. In 1750 an acting company arrived from London and hired a hall in Nassau Street for their performances of *Richard III*. After a five-month run with two performances a week the company disbanded, but the hall was used again, and was called the Nassau Street Theater.

4

In 1753 it was rebuilt by the Hallam family, who operated it until the following year. It was converted into a church in 1758. Three years later the Chapel Street Theater was built, only to be destroyed in 1764 by a mob unsympathetic to that form of amusement. Despite this, the John Street Theater — on John Street close to Broadway — opened in 1767, survived through the Revolution as the sometime Theater Royal, and later often entertained George Washington when New York was the Federal capital. The John Street was converted into a carriage factory in 1798.

The first New York theater with architectural and cultural pretensions was the Park Theater, on Park Row (3). The architects were Joseph and Charles Mangin, Joseph later collaborating in the design of City Hall across the street. The theater, begun in 1795, opened in 1798 with a performance of *As You Like It*. It burned down in 1820, was rebuilt, then burned down again in 1848, to be replaced by commercial buildings. Meanwhile a number of rivals had appeared: the Water Street Theater, the Grove Street Theater, Vauxhall Gardens, the New Olympic, and the Anthony Street Theater, where Edmund Kean made his New York debut in 1820. The most serious rival to the Park

was the Chatham Garden Theater (4), erected in 1824 (architect unknown). It subsequently changed its name to Blanchard's Amphitheater, since it was mostly devoted to comedy and light opera. The Park continued to hold on to its fashionable audience, however, and the unprofitable Chatham Garden was converted out of existence in 1832. By that time Niblo's Garden and Theater had been built (see page 47), a popular place with a long life in its several incarnations. In 1866 it was the scene of the first run of *The Black Crook*, the ancestor of modern musicals.

The Bowery Theater, at 46 Bowery, was designed by Ithiel Town and opened in 1826 as the New-York Theater. Early Living Newspaper-type productions were staged there; one in 1859, two weeks after the execution of John Brown, was called *The Insurrection, or Kansas and Harper's Ferry.* The Bowery was gutted by fire four times, but each time the exterior, considered a marvel of architectural beauty, remained safe. In 1879 it was rechristened the Thalia, and its columniated facade was later partially hidden by the Third Avenue El (6). Along with the Castle Garden theater (see page 96) it was considered one of the two great theatrical landmarks of old New York — until demolished in the early 20th century.

While the Nassau Street and Chatham Garden theaters were converted into churches, A. T. Stewart's Broadway Athenaeum (5) was a theater made from a church, remodeled in 1865 by J. H. Hackett. It operated under various managers as Daly's New Fifth-Avenue Theater, Fox's Broadway Theater, The Globe, and finally as the New Théâtre Comique when it was run by Harrigan & Hart. It stood at 728–30 Broadway opposite Waverly Place until it burned down in 1884.

The Théâtre Français opened in 1866 on 14th Street, west of Sixth Avenue. After some French-language productions it changed management and names several times (11). The street facade was unique. Its double portico, which provided protection for the audience at both lobby and gallery levels, was a handsome and distinguishing feature, even after it had been marred by fire escapes (the canopy over the sidewalk — less electric signs — appears to have been there from the start). As the Civic Repertory, it was run by Eva Le Gallienne from 1926 until 1932, devoted mainly to modern classic dramas. When the Repertory's subsidy gave out, the enterprise was discontinued and the building was ultimately demolished.

Other historically important downtown theaters were Tripler Hall and Wallack's. Tripler Hall, on Broadway opposite Bond Street, was built to serve for Jenny Lind's American debut (which, however, took place at Castle Garden instead, because Tripler Hall was not finished). It was later known as the New-York Theater, the Metropolitan Opera-House, Laura Keene's Varieties, and the Winter Garden,

suffering some fires between transformations. As the Winter Garden it burned to the ground in 1867. The famous Wallack's, the second theater of that name to be run by the Wallack family, was on Broadway and 13th Street. It opened in 1861 and had great popularity for twenty years because of the management's high production standards. In 1881 the name was changed to the Germania, and in 1883 it became called the Star. It was later pulled down, but by this time the Bowery Era of the New York stage had long since ended.

Italian opera was first heard in America at the Park Theater on November 29, 1825. The opera was *The Barber of Seville*. Lorenzo da Ponte, Mozart's great librettist (exiled from Venice and teaching at Columbia) promoted the first New York building devoted to opera — the 1833 Italian Opera House, at the southwest corner of Leonard and Church Streets. But the company's failure caused the building to be soon used as a playhouse. The same fate befell

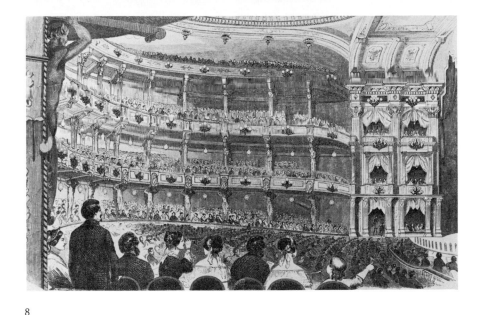

8

Palmo's Opera House which opened in 1844. The Astor Place Opera House, built by private subscription, opened in 1847 with *Ernani*. A year later it too became a playhouse, the scene of the Astor Place Riot in 1849 in which over twenty people were killed. In this incident Forrest, an American tragedian, was favored against his great English rival, Macready. When Forrest, as Macbeth, came to the line, "What purgative drug will scour these English hence?" the audience stopped the performance with cheering, and the uproar began.

The Academy of Music, at the northeast corner of 14th Street and Irving Place, was the first opera house at which opera remained popular. It was built in 1854 (7), burned down in 1866, and was rebuilt in 1868. The interior view (8), from *Ballou's Pictorial Drawing-Room Companion*, is described in the text: "The prevailing color is white, relieved by gold and crimson velvet. Let the reader look upon the engraving, and imagine every line in the picture to be a gold stripe, with the brilliant effect of a thousand gas lights shining thereupon, the private and stage boxes upholstered in the richest manner — and he may perhaps form some faint conception of the magnificent *ensemble* of this interior. Spacious and commodious, it is admirably adapted for seeing and hearing. The seats are all single, and constructed on the plan of those in the Boston and European theaters, the seat being so hinged that when the sitter rises it folds up against the back, allowing 'ample room and verge enough' to move about and make one's exit without inconvenience. The house will seat about four thousand comfortably." The opening of the Metropolitan Opera House in 1883 (see page 226), built by a corporation consisting largely of people who were unable to get boxes at the Academy of Music, put the Academy out of fashion. It was sold, altered for straight plays, and ultimately replaced by an office building.

After the 1866 fire at the Academy of Music, Samuel N. Pike of Cincinnati built an opera house in New York which opened in 1868. Pike's Opera House, at the northwest corner of Eighth Avenue and 23rd Street, was sold to Jim Fisk and Jay Gould the following year, and renamed the Grand Opera House (9, 10). It finally became a movie theater and survived until recently.

Among other New York operatic ventures, perhaps the best remembered were launched by Oscar Hammerstein at two separate Manhattan Opera Houses, built in 1892 and 1910. Both efforts were short-lived.

In 1909 the elegant New Theater was opened at Central Park West and 62nd Street (12), designed by Carrère and Hastings. The monumental lobby (13) and auditorium (14), reminiscent in style of the same

9

10

11

architects' New York Public Library, became the home in 1913–15 of yet another effort to rival the Met. The theater was renamed the Century Opera House. Later it was demolished to make way for the Century Apartments.

Until very recently, when thrust stages and arena theaters came back into vogue, there were only three basic types of theater built in modern times, and New York had some outstanding representatives of all three. There was the playhouse, with a somewhat narrow proscenium and overhanging balconies; the opera house, with a wider stage, bigger audience capacity and shallow galleries or boxes; and, created in the 20th century, there was the movie house. New York's Radio City Music Hall, the Paramount, the Roxy ("the Cathedral of the Motion Picture") and other film palaces were built with full stages, gridirons and wings for variety shows as well as screen entertainment, but even so they were characteristic movie theaters, a new type. Sight line angles had to be narrower because the audience could not be ranged along the sides. The pictures, at first silent and later amplified, allowed the auditorium to be far deeper than before. In these theaters for the first time the eye and ear of the observer were freed from the limitations

12

13

set by actors' voices and their size on stage. The house audiences could be immense. But the most significant new aspect of movie theaters was the appearance chosen, the impression to be made. They were often designed as treasure palaces, their interiors heaped high with exotic plaster riches.

New York movie houses departed from the scope of the nickelodeon in 1912 when Adolph Zukor imported the four-reel picture *Queen Elizabeth*. Its financial success led to *Quo Vadis*, an eight-reeler, which was shown at the Astor Theater for twenty-two consecutive weeks in 1913 at a one dollar top price. The Astor was a playhouse. The need for a more suitable theater was evident, and the following year Mitchell Mark opened the Strand Theater, designed for long film presentations. The Knickerbocker Theater, put up by the Triangle Film Corporation, soon followed, as well as the old Rialto and the Rivoli. These

last two were the promotional efforts of Samuel L. Rothapfel, who called himself Roxy. In 1919 he built the Capitol Theater on Broadway (most of the new movie palaces were around Times Square), then hailed as the largest theater in the world. The Paramount, the Roxy and the Music Hall were built subsequently. Booking records of the New York picture palaces ("four smash weeks at the Roxy") became potent sales statistics to regional exhibitors, and for most of their lives the huge movie theaters operated as no-profit presentation houses for Hollywood film companies. After World War II, when foreign films and independent production drained the powers of the big companies, the picture palaces started to go. The Roxy has already been demolished to make way for offices and a hotel garage, and the Paramount is being torn apart for conversion to store and office space.

15

16

17

One of the typical New York neighborhood movie theaters was Loew's 72nd Street, opened in 1932 as part of the Loew's chain which showed Metro-Goldwyn-Mayer films. The lobby (15), the mezzanine promenade (16) and the auditorium (17) were gorgeously decorated with gilded forms perhaps reminiscent of Angkor Wat to the architect, Thomas W. Lamb, or perhaps even more remotely inspired — another setting for the Big Screenplay, for the recherché pleasures of the world. The 72nd Street was demolished in 1961 when Loew's found that the land was more valuable than the theater.

As the most fashionable hotels, restaurants and residential addresses had done, playhouses also moved uptown. "The legitimate theater" found its new home "on Broadway," a west side area that began at about 34th Street and later centered itself at about 45th Street. Oscar Hammerstein built the opulent Olympia Theater on the east side of Broadway between 44th and 45th Streets. It was a vast entertainment palace which contained a concert hall, theater, roof garden and oriental cafe, and was an almost instant financial disaster. It then changed its name to the Lyric. Parts of the virtually unrecognizable carcass of the building survive in the Criterion Theater.

The Casino Theater (18), "one of the picturesque buildings of New-York City," according to King's 1893 *Handbook of New York*, was on the southeast corner of Broadway and 39th Street, "a fine illustration of the Arabesque or Moorish style of architecture." The Casino was built in 1882 to be a concert hall but usually played comic opera. The auditorium and roof garden were Arabesque or Moorish as well, fully detailed by Kimball & Wisedell, the architects. The Shuberts took over the house in 1902. It suffered a fire in 1905, but the famous theater survived until 1930. The Fulton Theater on West 46th Street (19), never destroyed but substantially altered as the present Helen Hayes Theater, was similarly designed for external appearance and street effect. It opened in 1911 as a theater-restaurant featuring the "Folies Bérgère." The Earl Carroll Theater, like the Ziegfeld on Sixth Avenue (see page 215), was devised to suit an audience who came to see girls glorified in ostrich feathers. The lobby ticket counter (20), once just inside its Broadway entrance, was a perfect model of the now-lost Broadway called the Great White Way.

18   19

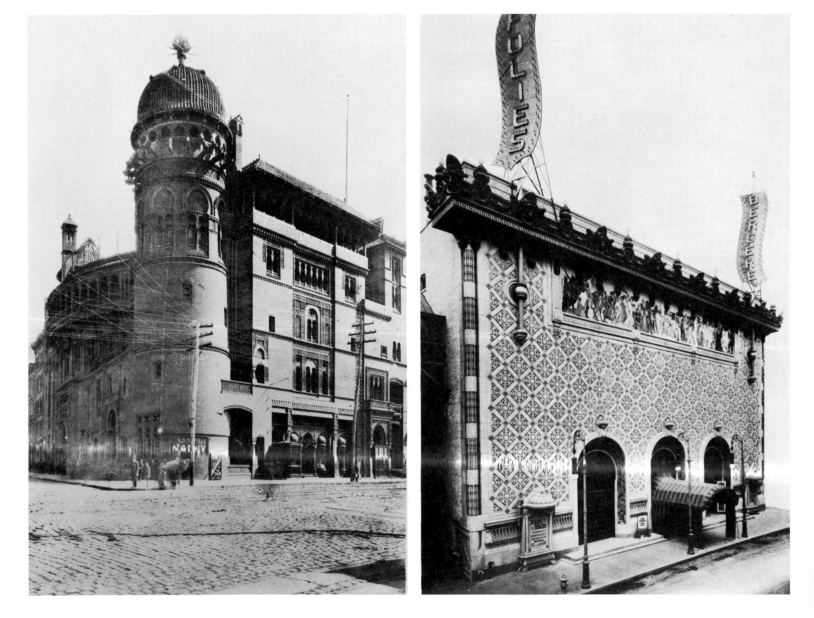

CIVIC ARCHITECTURE.

Buildings highly adapted to use are a recent development, coming from the modern idea that architectural form ought to be determined by the activities within. Architects speak of "building types" when similar interior activities make buildings resemble each other. Contemporary libraries resemble other libraries, not banks or schools.

But when architecture first became a fit subject for scholarship, distinctions according to building type were not thought to be particularly important — partly because activities were less specialized, partly because the architects lacked aesthetic license to express differences. From the Renaissance almost to the present, architectural historians treated buildings as formal expressions of primarily social or environmental import. Buildings were first categorized as either religious or secular. After that, the broad architectural subdivisions were Military, Civil and Domestic. This followed the idea that the most important consideration determining the appearance of a building was whether it was predominantly public or private. While a library, a bank and a school — being all public buildings — could look much alike, it was naturally important to make fine distinctions among palaces.

Most of New York's civic architecture was built primarily to be Civil Architecture. The buildings are not straightforward types so much as they are public buildings, designed to be well-mannered elements of a general municipal environment. In this sense, such things as deliberate monumentality, use of ornament, and eclectic formal styles should be seen not as shallow "facade architecture" but as aspects of a quite different aesthetic — attempts at concordant building in the public view. The fact that New York, like most cities, has had a predominance of such buildings may explain something about the agreeable if unremarkable overall character they have provided, and the feeling of loss and disruption in the city when they vanish.

The Croton Reservoir, Fifth Avenue from 40th to 42nd Streets, built 1839–43 with James Renwick employed as building Clerk-of-the-Works. The granite walls were forty-four and a half feet high. The reservoir was widely held, along with the first Tombs Prison, to be one of the two finest examples of "Egyptian architecture" in the country. People could parade around the rim by day or night for a bird's-eye view of the city. It was demolished in 1899–1900 to make way for the New York Public Library.

FEDERAL HALL.   From both an architectural and a historical point of view, Federal Hall might well have been the greatest national landmark had it survived. It stood on the northeast corner of Wall and Nassau Streets, on a site now occupied by the old Sub-Treasury building. Federal Hall was first built in 1699 as a new city hall. In 1788–89 it was substantially altered by Major Pierre Charles L'Enfant, one of Lafayette's officers — the same man who later did the plan of Washington, D.C. The remodeled Hall, shown in this print, had a facade much like Inigo Jones's unexecuted London design of 1617 for the Star Chamber. Yet when the remodeling was complete, it was taken as a polemic of French taste and became the beginning of the Federal style that flourished with Jefferson's approval and encouragement. The Hall was the scene of the first Congress after the Constitution, of Washington's election as President, and of his inauguration on April 30, 1789, which took place on the balcony. As he kissed the Bible after taking the oath of office, a flag was shown at the cupola to signal the firing of all the guns at the Battery and the ringing of all the bells in the city. When Congress transferred to Philadelphia, Federal Hall once again became City Hall, which it remained until the present city hall was completed in 1812.

GOVERNMENT HOUSE. In New York, Washington had lived in borrowed houses on Cherry Street and Broadway. An opportunity for building an official residence presented itself in 1789 when the state legislature decided upon the destruction of old Fort Amsterdam, leaving the site clear for a new public building. With its Ionic porch and decorated windows, Government House (attributed to James Robinson) was rather more Georgian than Federalist in character. It became the New York governor's mansion when the federal government moved away in August, 1790. After 1798 it was used as a hotel, as government offices, and as a custom house. The state tried to sell the property to New York City in May, 1812, but since the proposed transaction stipulated that the land could not be resold for private purposes, the city council took no interest, while that same month rapaciously ordering the sale at auction of Federal Hall, which the purchaser immediately tore down. The state amended its Government House offer in 1813, arranging its sale subject only to the soon-to-expire public lease. The city then bought it, and in 1815 bagged its profit by selling off the property in seven parcels. Government House was burned and demolished.

FIRE AND SHOT TOWERS. In the days of wood and masonry construction fire was the greatest civic problem, and the City of New York built a number of towers to serve as fire watch and alarm stations. One of these was shown in a contemporary magazine (1). According to the description: "This curious structure is situated in 33rd Street [the picture caption says 43rd Street], near its junction with Ninth Avenue. It was erected in 1851, by Messrs. Bogardus & Hoppin, builders in iron . . . One of the most notable points in the construction of this tower, was the drilling of the rock for the insertion of . . . anchorage shafts. The drilling was accomplished by means of machinery invented for the purpose. The lower part of the cavities drilled are larger than at the surface, so that the lower ends of the shafts, each being split, are, by the ingenious insertion of a wedge, made to spread, and are thus immovably imbedded in the rock. The cost of the tower was $6,000 . . . The Corporation of New York are now erecting a second fire tower, similar to the above, near the corner of Macdougal and Spring Streets." The

1   2

92

usefulness of fire towers was largely supplanted by a telegraph alarm system established in the late 1850s and a paid New York Fire Department in 1865.

James Bogardus, the builder of the fire tower shown, was a manufacturer of grinding machinery, and an inventor and popularizer of a complete cast-iron building system (see page 166). Among his other works were shot towers (2) — not really civic, except in an ornamental sense (though they were sometimes used for fire watch stations). Gunshot was made by splashing molten lead through screens at the top of a tower. The droplets then cooled into spheres as they fell through the air. Bogardus's shot towers, of which two were built in the 1850s in New York, were cast iron load-bearing structures with masonry infilling, the first true skeleton structures in the modern world. One at 63–65 Centre Street survived until 1908 (3), when it was torn down during subway construction.

3

ST. LUKE'S HOSPITAL.   Many of New York's largest
hospitals are private institutions. St. Luke's, the leading Protestant Episcopal
hospital, was founded on a site on West 54th Street and Fifth Avenue by
the Reverend William A. Muhlenberg in 1854; John W. Ketch, architect.
All the parts of the building in the photograph — including the chapel between
the two towers — were open in 1858 on their large grassy plot. But since
hospitals notoriously require ever-improving facilities and an expanding
plant, the present site of St. Luke's on Morningside Drive was chosen, and
competition-winner Ernest Flagg began supervising construction of the new
buildings in 1893. In 1896 the painted brick institution on Fifth Avenue was
demolished.

TOMPKINS MARKET ARMORY. The Seventh Regiment, which gained some prominent friends after the Astor Place Riot, was unified under one roof in 1860 in the Tompkins Market Armory. This was a handsome structure on the east side of the Bowery between 6th and 7th Streets, the first building erected by New York City with special facilities for an individual military unit. Within the iron frame, the first floor was a market, the second floor Company rooms, and the third floor (under an arched vault, an earlier roof structure than the timber trusses shown in this 1911 demolition photograph) was the drill room. The building's multiple use was an outstanding idea for maintaining the property's economy; but the Regiment moved to its own armory on Park Avenue in 1880 (see page 218).

CASTLE GARDEN: THE AQUARIUM.   The Battery was originally an artillery position. It was supplemented about 1807 by the Southwest Battery, a fortification 300 feet offshore, later called Castle Clinton after being improved by John McComb, Jr. When the federal government took over Governor's Island for use as a military base in 1822, the Battery properties were ceded to New York. The city used the Battery as a promenade and parade ground. Across its connecting drawbridge, Castle Clinton was made into a public assembly room and renamed Castle Garden.

Beginning with the 1824 reception for the return of Lafayette to the United States, Castle Garden established itself as New York's most eminent civic hall. It was there that Barnum arranged Jenny Lind's fabulous American debut (1) on September 11, 1850. The building had outstanding qualities for diverse uses (2), and in 1896, after a term as the U.S. Immigrant Station, it accommodated the New York Aquarium. Landfill had meanwhile gradually absorbed the island into Battery Park (3).

After over fifty years of popularity, the Aquarium was unwisely closed and moved to far less accessible Coney Island. Since losing its use, the old building has been "restored" back to its presumed earliest condition, and is now called "Castle Clinton National Monument."

1

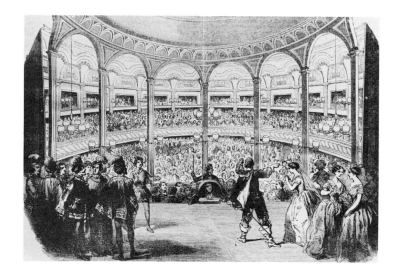

2

3

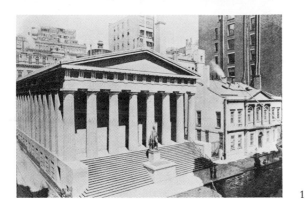

1

THE ASSAY OFFICE.   This building was erected at 30 Wall Street in 1823 to be the New York branch of the Bank of the United States; Martin E. Thompson, architect. After the failure of that institution it served two other banks. It was bought by the government and made into a U.S. Assay Office, where gold and silver were refined and made into bullion from 1854 to 1912. Until demolished in 1915, it stood next to the Sub-Treasury building (1, left). The esteemed facade was re-erected in 1924 at the Metropolitan Museum.

2

1

COLUMBIA'S MIDTOWN CAMPUS.   Columbia has existed on three sites.   From 1754 to 1857 it was at Church Street and Park Place (as King's College and a Tory hotbed it had been disbanded during the Revolution). From 1857 it used some buildings in midtown near a legacy to Columbia from an alumnus, the Elgin Botanical Garden estate. The library, built in 1884, was on 49th Street (1, right), and at the corner of 50th Street and Madison was Hamilton Hall of 1880 (2) — "Collegiate Gothic" buildings by Charles C. Haight. The third site, on Morningside Heights, was acquired in 1892, and a few years later the midtown campus was abandoned.

2

FIREHOUSE.   In 1819 the New York volunteer fire brigades began to abandon buckets in favor of a great improvement in fire-fighting equipment — the hose. Since hoses had to be dried after use, the need for specially designed firehouses was an economically significant reason for the establishment of the municipal fire department. This classic firehouse, with hose drying tower, was on Park Avenue and 135th Street, until demolished to make way for the East River Drive.

COTTON EXCHANGE. New York's strength as a financial capital is largely based on its exchanges, where stocks, bonds, and commodities are freely traded. The Stock Exchange — said to have begun under a buttonwood tree — has expanded and moved several times, but the Cotton Exchange was organized only in 1871. This building, designed for the Exchange by George B. Post, was completed in 1885 at William and Beaver Streets, where a new one now stands. Besides providing a thirty-five foot high exchange room and a clubhouse, the Cotton Exchange adopted standards, settled disputes, and established commercial principles. Within Post's bit of Chambord with the characteristic downtown-Manhattan corner entrance, cotton traders were first made to feel at home in New York.

THE PRODUCE EXCHANGE.   George B. Post's most noted work may have been the Western Union building (see page 162), but his most notable one was the Produce Exchange (1), finished in 1884 at Bowling Green on Beaver Street. The mammoth structure was faced with rich dark red brick, which later provided a striking contrast to the white stone building and sculpture of the Custom House (2 — and see page 223). Terra cotta bas-reliefs on the Produce Exchange were of the produce traded within. The building had a true iron skeleton, finished a year before Jenney's Home Insurance building in Chicago. The main hall on the second floor (3) measured 220 by 144 feet, with heights of $47\frac{1}{2}$ feet to the ceiling and 60 feet to the skylight. The Produce Exchange, one of the best buildings in New York, was replaced after 1957 by one of the worst.

1

2

3

JAILS.   Historically, jails have been a great social convenience, and it was long considered to be of public benefit to put them on display. While the effectiveness of the cautionary lesson may be open to doubt, there is, as Piranesi knew, no question of the effectiveness of prisons in architectural expression. From Loches on the Loire to the Allegheny County Jail in Pittsburgh, jails have presented themselves to the world as sheer monuments — formal exhibition objects of massive geometrical masonry.

New York has had no buildings as terror-haunted as Loches or as awe-inspiring as Richardson's Pittsburgh jail, but the prisons built have nevertheless offered citizens some obvious expressionism. The first Tombs Prison (2), by architect John Haviland, was finished in 1838 on the filled-in Collect Pond; the choice of site was a nice symbolic touch, since a pre-Revolutionary gibbet stood on an island there. The name arose from its associations — although the neo-Egyptian architecture was more reminiscent of a temple than a tomb.

The Tombs gave way in 1897 to the new Tombs on the same site (3), a fortress which had 320 cells and two chapels. It was replaced about 1947 by the new Criminal Courts building at Leonard and Centre Streets.

The Jefferson Market Prison (1), at Greenwich Avenue and 10th Street, was a minor city prison used for temporary detention, and typical of other small jails attached to police courts. Its significance lies in the fact that the prison and courthouse (built 1874–77 by Frederick Clark Withers and Calvert Vaux), together with a market and firehouse, were probably New York's first comprehensive public building group, though not simultaneously planned. Everything except the courthouse and its clocktower was demolished in 1927 to make way for a new prison, the Women's House of Detention. Since this has lately come under attack as being an outmoded institution, it seems that the idea of discipline as an architectural problem in penal fortification will continue to wither away.

1   2   3

1

THE CITY HALL POST OFFICE.   It may be only modern sophistication to think that the Post Office between Broadway and Park Row (1) was a handsome and vigorous building, because almost from the first it was considered a municipal eyesore. It became the city's main post office in 1875, when postal services moved from the old Middle Dutch Church building (see page 147). A. B. Mullett, the government architect, had done his best to see that the building had modern and adequate facilities — such as a pneumatic system that linked the building with other stations, and loading bays along one side which were afterward covered with canopies (4).

What was impressive about the building in a formal sense was its relentless fragmentation of architectural elements (2), dramatically superior even to the same architect's State, War and Navy Department

3

2

4

building in Washington, finished the same year. But its most compelling trait was the way the Post Office played against City Hall (3), a building of about the same volume. The Post Office served to enclose the south side of City Hall Park, and even the mistake of having the loading docks on the north side of the Post Office did not spoil the principle of the neat urban square. When Cass Gilbert's Woolworth Tower was built (3, tallest building), the Post Office not only made it seem taller, but it kept City Hall from appearing as an isolated dwarf.

Even though City Hall Park was somewhat extended after the Post Office was demolished in 1939, this urban scene was, on balance, much weakened by the new long view down Broadway and the sight of some clumsy highway engineering at the intersection where the Post Office had been.

THE MUSEUM OF MODERN ART, STAGE I.   The Museum, at 11 West 53rd Street, was a glistening intruder in 1939, when it shattered a block of brownstones with its crisp design and careful scale. New additions by Philip Johnson are in character, but not unified with the original street wall. The Museum has consequently lost the contrast with the street which was the explicit visual virtue of the building by Philip L. Goodwin and Edward D. Stone.

GREAT HOUSES.

Compared to other cities, a relatively large number of people in New York have been able to accumulate an enormous amount of wealth. During the 19th century there were fortunes to be made in a growing country, and in a growing city (with real estate still cheap) prestige could be bought. These mutually agreeable circumstances led to palace-building of a quantity without precedent in any city of the world. Most of the financiers, landlords, merchants and operators who amassed fortunes in the city built great houses. And even many entrepreneurs whose profits were made elsewhere built New York *Stadtpalasts* for their families. Within a scant three generations Manhattan changed from a mostly rural, certainly provincial city into an imperial capital. The great houses at first lined downtown streets, then midtown Fifth Avenue, and finally upper Fifth Avenue and avenues on the West Side.

Support for the mansions of the rich at first seems hardly an important civic responsibility. Yet the family palaces of the 19th century were unique New York elements, authentic manifestations of a time and place. Having created some fashionable streets, many great houses later became early victims of rising property values. Those that remain, particularly along Fifth Avenue, ought to be preserved — either to be turned over to institutions sympathetic to their character, or in the best examples (as the English National Trust has done to many houses) maintained intact with furnishings, and opened to the public.

House of Cornelius Vanderbilt II — the carriage entrance, facing the Plaza. The building was begun with the southern section in 1880 and was enlarged in 1894 at this northern end, after designs by George B. Post and certain details by Richard M. Hunt. The house had thirty servants. It was demolished in 1927 to make way for a department store. Only the north gates remain, re-erected in Central Park at 105th Street.

THE APTHORPE MANSION.   Charles Ward Apthorpe, a Colonial lawyer, built this house in about 1764 on his 200 acre farm on the Bloomingdale Road. The portico doorway opened into a hall the full depth of the house, large enough for a cotillion party. Walls, mantels and ceilings in all the main rooms were paneled in English brown oak: in an era of costly transportation, evidence of the owner's great wealth. The mansion was headquarters at different times for Clinton, Howe and Washington. It was later converted into a tavern, which stood near 91st Street and Columbus Avenue. The building was torn down in 1892 when a row of apartment houses was built on the site.

DORIC MANSION.   The Greek Revival and the Gothic Revival were individual modes of what has been called Romantic Classicism, an attitude where cultural ideals were symbolized by the inventive re-use of distant architectural forms. The vanished Anderson house on Throgs Neck, the Bronx, was built about 1830; probably by Josiah R. Brady, architect. To those inspired by classical culture, the Doric order used was primitive and wild. It was an early Greek figure, appropriate for an almost solitary landscape.

GOTHIC VILLA.   Alexander Jackson Davis, for a time a partner of Ithiel Town, was an architect who arrived in New York from Connecticut in the early 19th century. At first doing odd jobs in art — he made the drawing of the Doric Mansion on page 113 — he soon began to get a great deal of architectural work. As an example of one side of the double ideal of Romantic Classicism, nothing could be clearer than the house he did for W. C. H. Waddell, illustrated in 1844. Since the house — at the northwest corner of 37th Street and Fifth Avenue — was a suburban villa, it was appropriate for it to be casually Picturesque. The house was demolished in 1856 to make way for a church, which was in turn destroyed in 1938.

GREEK PALACE. The other side of the Romantic Classical ideal aimed at the Sublime, and many houses were designed like Greek temples, a fancy initiated in America by Thomas Jefferson and Benjamin Latrobe. A. J. Davis's house for the wealthy ship builder John Cox Stevens, now also lost, was a Corinthian-columned affair which was built about 1849 near Murray Street and West Broadway. Since it was a town house, it needed to be starched and lordly. Of it, the contemporary diarist Philip Hone wrote: "The Palais Bourbon in Paris, Buckingham Palace in London and the Sans Souci at [sic] Berlin are little grander than this residence of a simple citizen of our Republican city . . ."

JOHN C. STEVENS. COLLEGE PLACE, N.Y.   A. J. DAVIS. ARCHITECT.

PRIME HOUSE.   With wood the commonest construction material for country estates, large houses often took their form as much from the logic of building in timber as from the modes of Gothic or Greek Revival. The old Prime house was built in 1800, overlooking the East River at the foot of 89th Street. The pictures show opposite sides, probably the driveway frontage (1) and the eastern river frontage (2).

2

BREVOORT HOUSE. One of the best-known mansion houses was this one for Henry Brevoort at the northwest corner of 9th Street and Fifth Avenue, built in 1834 and probably designed by the firm of Ithiel Town and A. J. Davis. Although it was freestanding — in fact there was a garden entrance on one side and a curved window bay on the other — its crisp design could have made it a model for later New York row houses. But the building's plainness was not simplicity. Its Greek key cornice ornament and the paneled front wall were original ideas. In 1925, with the name temporarily assured of survival in the Brevoort Hotel (see page 42), the Brevoort house was torn down to make way for another hotel.

HALF AND HALF HOUSE.   Before iron was widely used in construction, the difference between a wood and a masonry house was quite small. In both cases, except in the unlikely event that masonry vaulting supported the floors, all the internal spans and usually all interior walls were of timber. Only the exterior walls might be masonry. The difference in construction between the brick and the clapboard halves of the Colonel Kopper house, which stood on 124th Street between Third and Lexington Avenues, was really only skin deep — but it would be hard to imagine a blunter demonstration of the use of expensive materials for the front part of a building only. The house dated from 1790, and was by Johann Hermann Raub.

WHEELOCK HOUSE.   Eclecticism, a philosophical concept orig-
inating in France in the 1830s, described a system of thought composed of
elements selected from other systems. The idea was internationally adapted
to architecture, in the belief that a rational selection of historical forms could
be assembled to create a whole building which would then be appropriate for
modern use. The house built about 1860 by William A. Wheelock in New
York at 661 West 158th Street was an enthusiastic example of the Eclectic
mode — the ogee roofs, inventive ornament, circular and flattened window
heads were all vital characteristics. It survived on Riverside Drive only
through the late 1930s.

FIFTH AVENUE, NORTH FROM 65TH STREET. By 1898, Fifth Avenue from 46th Street to 72nd Street was an almost uninterrupted mile and a half of palazzi, chateaux and fortresses, bordering Central Park. Richard Morris Hunt's house for Mrs. John Jacob Astor and William B. Astor is at the right in the photograph, and beyond that lived Haights, Goulds, Millses, Belmonts, on and on to the north — a visual summary of free enterprise and the history of architecture. This staggering parade of wealth has been drastically altered by the replacement of most of the buildings by tall apartment houses.

120

1

VANDERBILT HOUSES. By 1880, the Vanderbilt fortune was the greatest ever amassed in America. William Henry Vanderbilt, son of the Commodore, had two great houses built for him by Gustav and Christian Herter on Fifth Avenue from 51st to 52nd Streets (1, left). The twin houses, built in 1880–84, were divided by an atrium that separated the W. H. Vanderbilt residence from that of his two sons-in-law, Elliott F. Shepard and William D. Sloane. Across 52nd Street to the north was Richard Morris Hunt's house for William Kissam Vanderbilt (1, right), William Henry's son, built 1879–81. Concurrently, Cornelius Vanderbilt II (also son of William Henry) had the first part of George B. Post's

design under way for himself on 57th Street (see pages 24 and 111). It was said that $15,000,000 was expended on the building, decoration and furnishing of the Vanderbilt houses.

One of the specific objectives of the Vanderbilts was to build a more staggering house than A. T. Stewart had done (facing page). Considering their outlay, this was relatively easy. William Henry Vanderbilt had included in his house an art gallery (2) to which the public was admitted by card on Thursdays. The visual feast guests were able to enjoy within the gallery included exotic marbles, mother-of-pearl, glass, gold and polychrome — the room, according to a contemporary publication, was "an important element in cultivating the artistic taste of the metropolis."

The William K. Vanderbilt house was demolished in 1925, and the last half of the Vanderbilt twins vanished in 1947.

THE A. T. STEWART HOUSE.   Alexander Turney Stewart, celebrated as a tightwad and grouch, nevertheless contributed three notable buildings to New York: his hotel for working women which became the Park Avenue Hotel (see page 66), his department store (page 168), and his home, on the northwest corner of 34th Street and Fifth Avenue. The Stewart mansion, built in 1864–69 by John W. Kellum, architect of all three, was the least comely of the buildings — $3,000,000 of marble and Civil War-period pomp. The Grand Hall heading toward his art gallery was filled with unmistakably parvenu art. After the death of Stewart's widow the building was torn down in 1901 to make room for the old Knickerbocker Trust Company's bank.

MARY MASON JONES HOUSE.   Between 57th and 58th Streets on the east side of
Fifth Avenue was "Marble Row" (see page 26), a rich man's housing project planned by Mary Mason
Jones, whose banker father had paid the city $1500 for the site in 1825. The white marble houses were
built by the architect Robert Mook in 1867–69. Mrs. Jones herself occupied the corner house at 57th Street
shown in this photograph. The house, the owner, and Mrs. Paran Stevens, the next occupant, all figured
in Edith Wharton's fiction in slight disguise. By the '90s the commercial possibilities of the row had
become irresistible, and the corner pavilion at 58th Street was made into a bank. The handsome row
vanished altogether in 1929.

124

THE SENATOR CLARK HOUSE.   One of the more ephemeral of New York's expendable buildings was the solid-looking William A. Clark house on the northeast corner of 77th Street and Fifth Avenue. Senator Clark of Montana, a "copper king," hired the sophisticated architects Lord, Hewlett & Hull and K. M. Murchison to come to terms with his desires; a proposition that took six years and ultimately also involved H. Deglane of Paris as a consultant.   The extraordinary result of their labors was completed in 1901, a building made mostly of white granite, and said to contain 130 rooms. The house immediately fell under attack in gossip and print, twice in *Collier's* alone the following year, which printed satirical poems about its alleged vulgarity.   Only twenty-three years after it had been built, the improbable structure was demolished.

THE SCHWAB HOUSE.   Compared to Fifth Avenue, the allurement of Riverside Drive took longer to bloom and faded more quickly. Its charms included proximity to Morningside Heights ("the Acropolis of America" in the '90s), and a great west-facing view of the sunset behind the Hudson Palisades. Frederick Law Olmsted had sponsored the design for Riverside Park on land acquired by the city after 1872, and though at the turn of the century trees were still low and the Drive itself seemingly far too wide, many wealthy men had already responded to the attractiveness of the upper West Side.

This was the situation to which Charles M. Schwab committed himself when he built his enormous Riverside Drive mansion in 1902–06, with Maurice Hebert as architect. The property was the entire block north of 73rd Street. But the far West Side was borderland — a strip of valuable fortified houses with lines of communication only back to downtown; cut off even from nearby Central Park West, another affluent border. Between the two park edges multiple dwellings became overcrowded and run down, and Riverside Drive lost its chance of surpassing Fifth Avenue's demonstration of wealth. The Schwab house was empty in 1947 and has been replaced by an apartment house.

THE BROKAW MANSIONS   The greatest cry for preservation in New York arose in September, 1964, when the Brokaw mansions, houses at 984 Fifth Avenue, 1 East 79th Street, and 7 East 79th Street, were announced for demolition; and again in February, 1965, when the work of razing was begun on a weekend. The disposition of the old Brokaw property became an issue prominently discussed in New York newspapers and a number of magazines. The outcry was undoubtedly what at last induced the mayor to sign the law giving the Landmarks Commission legal powers, and that fact is the most distinguished landmark quality the Brokaw mansions ever had.

Isaac Vail Brokaw, a clothing manufacturer and real estate man, had the corner house built according to plans by Rose & Stone in 1887–88 (with roof off in the picture). He subsequently ordered two adjacent

houses to the north (1905, by Charles F. Rose) for two sons, and an adjacent house to the east for a daughter (1911), the architect H. Van Buren Magonigle. The northernmost house at 985 Fifth Avenue is still standing.

Apart from their considerable interior amenities, the only house of the group with a degree of real merit was Brokaw's first. There was dignity and rugged solidity in the old castle, though it was not nearly as skillful a design as Hunt's Vanderbilt chateau on 52nd Street (see page 121). The most important thing about the Brokaw mansions on the urban scene was the way they marked a very important corner. At the crossroads of Fifth Avenue and the 79th Street-Central Park Transverse, they made a reassuringly rich pile of masonry where one turned from East 79th Street up to the Metropolitan Museum.

THE NEW YORK ROW HOUSE.

As the gridiron of streets and the subway system extended, houses were built from block to block. The type of house favored by the speculative builders was attached to its neighbors. This row-house type allowed for great economies in land use, since many could be built side by side on narrow street frontage. The typical New York block dimension of 200 by 600 to 800 feet also permitted relatively deep buildings, each with a rear yard, on all four sides of the block. The corners suited larger developments.

The one-family row house was also very economical to build. Common walls which separated the houses carried the floor loads, and the walls were no further apart than necessary for cheap timber floor joist spans. Almost the only surfaces which could be called architectural problems were the front and rear walls. The rear wall was inevitably brick, but after the 1860s the finish material on the front was sometimes limestone and often brownstone, a type of sandstone usually obtained from a now played-out vein in New Jersey. While soft and easily eroded, brownstone could be patched and repaired with colored cement. Compared with the frequent treatment of terrace houses in London and Bath, there were few historic attempts in New York to visually combine ranges of row houses. The idea that many houses should be treated to look like one wide palace must have been taken as more appropriate for the side of a square than for a linear street. What could be called comprehensive design in New York merely amounted to the rough alignment of adjacent cornice heights and masonry stringcourses, while the limitations of height imposed by wall bearing and stair climbing also served to unify designs.

As one-family town houses, the New York row house seemed ideal. Wealthier families could have carriages and stables, but the liveability of the basic type was within reach of many. The row houses that remain are highly valued today, and are likely to increase further in value — both to the owners and to the city — as other resident types become ever more predominant.

Some typical speculative row houses near Lenox Avenue on West 133rd Street, about 1882. These were built for single-family occupancy according to a conventional plan. Within fifteen years most of the vacant sites had been filled with similar houses. Buildings of this type are rapidly vanishing all over the city.

LA GRANGE TERRACE ("COLONNADE ROW").   Lafayette Street was once Lafayette Place, a short, wide residential enclave, and only later city developments cut it into the commercial conduit that it is today. In 1830 it was comely enough to be a likely site for speculative development, and Seth Geer hired an architect to design nine houses for him there, running up to 47 Lafayette Place (now 434 Lafayette Street) and completed in 1833. The Terrace has often been attributed to A. J. Davis, but recent evidence suggests that it may have been the work of Robert Higham, an Albany architect associated with Philip Hooker.

Whoever the designer, there is persuasive reason to believe that he conceived of the twenty-eight free-standing Corinthian columns as an architectural ensemble. Like the columniated buildings of Playfair in Edinburgh, the Woods in Bath, or Smirke in London, La Grange Terrace (named after Lafayette's country home) was a unified work — as great as any of theirs for the simplicity of the architect's subject and the grandeur he gave it. The destruction of five-ninths of the Terrace in 1901 to make way for Wanamaker's warehouse can therefore be taken as the destruction of his intent. The rump four houses are now designated as Landmarks.

UNDERHILL'S COLONNADE BUILDINGS. In 1837 Brooklyn was another city, and in that period, long before the Brooklyn Bridge was built, New York was already an admirable sight from its high coast. The row of Greek Revival houses built around that time on Brooklyn's Columbia Heights near Middagh Street was perhaps influenced by La Grange Terrace, but the unifying beauty of its colonnade was here less of benefit to its occupants than it was a gift to the New Yorkers across the East River.

This picture was used as an advertisement for the houses, though the unexplained fire indicates its original purpose may have been different. Underhill's Colonnade, long gone, appeared in many views of the river scene.

HOUSES WITH PITCHED ROOFS. "A great number of excellent private dwellings are built of red painted brick, which gives them a peculiarly neat and clean appearance," a London visitor to New York wrote in 1819. The characteristic house was two or three stories high, sometimes twenty-five feet wide, two rooms deep, with a pitched roof and delicate dormers. These, built long before the Civil War, were at 512–514 Broome Street, and are now gone.

HOUSES WITH WOODEN PORCHES.   From the middle of the 19th century, roofs were sometimes metal, frequently flat or slightly pitched, and hidden behind a raised cornice. The row house got to be a higher building than it had generally been before. The gridiron street layout of the 1811 Commissioners' Plan was an accomplished fact. One effect of the gridiron was to insure that most house plots would be a uniform 100 feet deep. Another was that few houses would possess a vista. New York row houses consequently adapted themselves to site conditions by taking great account of available open space, both in developing the rear garden, and — sometimes — by increasing the privacy of the front. A way of doing this was by building on exterior porches, which also gave the standard double-room depth an extra space and dimension. Many Greenwich Village brick row houses had wooden porches, usually in the rear. The vanished "Cottage Row" shown, on Seventh Avenue between 12th and 13th Streets, had them in front (the row was built about 1850, and had ornamental railings which were removed in 1931). The houses were designed in a unit, as indicated by the dentil blocks uniformly under the cornice and the symmetrical projection of the center and end bays.

LONDON TERRACE.   The London Terrace houses, on the north side of 23rd Street between Ninth and Tenth Avenues, were designed for William Torrey in 1845 by A. J. Davis. They were uniformly pilastered to give the effect of a colonnade from one avenue to the other, and were set back about thirty-five feet from the street, with gardens in front. Similar buildings, known as "Chelsea Cottages," were on the 24th Street side of the block. This property was all eradicated by the block of flats that now bears the London Terrace name.

RHINELANDER GARDENS.   This row of houses was at 110–124 West 11th Street, between Sixth and Seventh Avenues. It was built in 1854 by James Renwick, architect also of Grace Church and St. Patrick's. Its tiers of cast-iron balconies unified the street facade much as did the columns of La Grange Terrace, or the wall pillars of London Terrace. In a way Rhinelander Gardens was even more prepossessing than those others, because its ironwork was the beautiful product of a machine technology, later called more and more into architectural use. The setback fronts of the houses were the result of the imperfect match of the old Greenwich Village street pattern with the upper Manhattan grid. Some deep fronts can still be seen on 11th Street, but the Rhinelander row was demolished in the late 1950s.

MANSARDED TERRACE.   The block of speculative row houses on Fifth Avenue between 55th and 56th Streets was a bit less grand, but otherwise similar in many ways to the mansions of "Marble Row" (see page 26); it was finished in the same year (1869), had mansard roofs, and was also clad in marble. This terrace was one story higher and was the work of a distinguished architect, the Danish-American Detlef Lienau. In addition to his use of the currently fancied roof shape, Lienau designed the various levels as superimposed architectural orders.

THE BROWNSTONES.   In *Things As They Are in America*, William Chambers, the Edinburgh publisher of *Chambers's Encyclopaedia*, said this about New York in 1853: "Wherever any of [the] older brick edifices have been removed, their place has been supplied by tenements [dwellings] built of brown sandstone; and it may be said that at present New York is in process of being renewed by this species of structure . . ." The older brick buildings were usually painted red with white joints (which was really more durable, since brownstone spalled in freezing weather). But the choice of brownstone for cladding the Vanderbilt twins (see page 121) finally confirmed the material's stylish supremacy. By the 1880s, New York had become a red and brown city as Bath was cream and London black and white. With the main brownstone quarries now no longer open, "brownstones" — the remaining terrace houses faced with the material — are quickly vanishing without an echo.

APARTMENT HOUSES.

Frank Lloyd Wright's Broadacre City project envisioned a place where everyone would have his separate house and plot. His design was a reaction to modern cities, where most people must live in multiple dwellings. High population densities, and hence apartment house developments, were inevitable under conditions where land values were increasing, transportation was poor, and rental accommodations were acceptable — the loss of a back yard and a personal front door to the street could be measured against the big advantages of apartment life, with its potential social vitality and convenient urban location. New York produced two noteworthy early models of apartment houses. One was a sort of communal palace, typified by the Dakota (which still stands, on Central Park West and 72nd Street). This building type had every comfort of a private great house but was developed in multiple form, and with the services of a grand hotel added. Extraordinary measures were taken to insure the privacy and isolation of separate suites, to make community life not too trying.

The other New York paradigm was the Old-Law tenement. In a sense this was also built as an accurate response to the requirements of life. Early "railroad flats" with only the end rooms receiving light and air succumbed to the Tenement House Law of 1879, the barely restrictive "old law." The demand for cheap housing led to the development of a special building form to suit the law, which exploited land and the adaptability of its inhabitants to the fullest. Since real estate was sold on the basis of street frontage, very deep narrow buildings were the most profitable. With the stair in the center, a long strip of rooms could be run from front to back on each side. These rooms became either two or four apartments per floor, with public toilets on the landing. The stairway and the shafts to let air and a little light down to the inside rooms gave the apartments a characteristic dumbbell-plan shape. Within the apartments one room opened directly into another. Front doors were often set at an angle to keep the public passageway at the minimum possible width.

These early multiple dwellings became characteristic New York types. When a refined apartment house design at last began to appear, a sort of compromise between the rich and poor extremes, the buildings were called French Flats, because there was no American precedent. The acceptance of French Flats by the public was historically significant. Their eventual profusion established middle-class urban society at a new density in American cities. The New York communal palaces and Old-Law tenements are now rapidly disappearing, elegant brontosauruses and grim pterodactyls among the more highly refined evolutionary building forms.

The Navarro Flats, Central Park South and Seventh Avenue, designed by Hubert, Pirsson & Co., built in 1882. To help reduce the fashionable prejudice toward apartment life, it was built and operated as a group of individual houses, known as the Madrid, Granada, Lisbon, Cordova, Barcelona, Valencia, Salamanca and Tolosa. It was destroyed to provide a site for a new building. The present Navarro Hotel is a namesake, down the block.

THE "OLD-LAW TENEMENTS."   New York is well rid of some of its vanishing buildings. When the new 1901 Tenement House Law was passed, there were about 86,000 buildings in the city which the new law declared substandard. They were mostly supreme exploitation properties. Under the old law, it was possible to build a house for $25,000 on a 25 by 100 foot lot that housed a dozen families, or two dozen in some neighborhoods. Moses King's 1893 *Handbook of New York City*, noting the wide distribution of tenements, pointed out that "In a single block between Avenue B and Avenue C and 2nd and 3rd Streets there are over 3,500 residents, and a smaller block on Houston Street contains 3,000 people, which is at the rate of 1,000,000 to the square mile." This density was achieved in buildings usually no more than six stories high, which makes the packing of people even more incredible than it would seem today. In 1891 the Board of Health found that two-thirds of the entire population of the city were living in tenements, according to King's *Handbook*. Some tenements were better than others (and "the city" before 1898 was not Greater New York), but it is clear that misery and overcrowding was the condition of the majority. Although the new law made such slum houses forbidden, the law was not retroactively effective on this better-lost aspect of New York. Immigration and other population pressures — as well as continued profitability — keep about half of the Old-Law tenements still intact today, such as most of those on Henry Street (1) and 100th Street (2).

1

STUDIO BUILDING.   There are various claims as to which building in New York was the first multiple dwelling, but undoubtedly the first building specialized to provide artists' studios — living quarters were included — was the Studio Building, at 51–55 West 10th Street, designed by Richard Morris Hunt (who was later responsible for the W. K. Vanderbilt house — page 121). Hunt was headmost in the procession of American architects to study at the École des Beaux-Arts, and he had returned from Paris just two years prior to construction of the Studio in 1857. His client was James Boorman Johnson, and the building became a virtual clubhouse of the Hudson River School. Its popularity was evident when it later became a cooperative, and the building's importance was the first demonstration that high, well-lit rooms would be welcome in New York apartments. After having housed John LaFarge, Frederick Church, and Winslow Homer (among scores of others), the Studio was demolished in 1954.

THE KNICKERBOCKER.   The Knickerbocker, now vanished, is said to have been one of New York's first cooperative apartment houses. It was on Fifth Avenue at 28th Street, built there when the Madison Square area was still fashionable. Ernest Flagg, architect of the building, was also the accomplished designer of the two Singer buildings (see pages 211 and 212) and the still extant Scribner's at 597 Fifth Avenue.

CHURCHES.

In recent years, as the pattern of urban settlement changed and quantities of New Yorkers moved off to the suburbs, church and synagogue leaders could be heard explaining church relocation moves by pointing out to the public that a religious establishment was not a *building* at all really, it was a *congregation*. This was fair warning that a church was soon to be sold. Though religious institutions are not taxed, central urban property represents a considerable frozen asset to a congregation seeking to establish itself elsewhere. Without the state interest in religion that operates in cities such as London and Rome, churches in New York have been subjected to the same economic imperatives and forces as corporations. Sanctified ground seems less sanctified when the real estate value soars. This problem has been a source of worry to St. Paul's Chapel on Broadway and Fulton Street, and to the Friends Meeting House at Gramercy Park (see page 203).

New York has had a quite remarkable number of fine churches and synagogues destroyed. Some of the most stylish period buildings in America — the Greek and Gothic Revival churches on this and the facing page, for example, and such authentic masterpieces as St. John's — have been sold and demolished. It would probably be beyond the scope of urban conservation policy to arrange for the continuous use of churches that are no longer serving a local population, but a preservation program that is supported by church groups would be a welcome change in attitude. Churches were deeply significant buildings in the early formation of New York, and are still essential elements of the public patrimony.

The Jones Chapel (1), on East 64th Street, was built about 1830. The Mount Washington Church (2), at Broadway and Dyckman Street, was built in 1844 and enlarged in 1856. Each building was an elegantly characteristic example, in timber, of a revival mode. Both are now gone.

1

2

THE OLD BRICK CHURCH.   The Brick Presbyterian Church by John McComb, Sr. was on the northeast corner of Beekman and Nassau Streets. Its picture here, from *Frank Leslie's Illustrated* in 1856, was engraved on the occasion of rumors of its imminent destruction to make way for a post office. The land then was "probably the most valuable in the city." The post office deal apparently fell through, but the congregation managed to sell the property to the *New York Times* which put up a building on the site in 1857–58. The old Brick Church had been there since 1767.

THE MIDDLE DUTCH CHURCH.   Revival modes were at their most spectacular in New York's religious buildings. The old Elm Street Synagogue, for example, was a three-bay Doric temple, on top of which was a perfect little English Perpendicular cupola. The Middle Dutch Church, however — finished in 1839 on Lafayette Place, near La Grange Terrace — was a single-mindedly classic Greek Revival church by Isaiah Rogers, perhaps his best work (see also page 68). Unfortunately for posterity, the Dutch Reformed (Collegiate) denomination was wealthy enough to move as frequently as the neighborhood ran down. This church's forerunner was built in 1729 at Nassau Street, later became the Post Office, and was demolished in 1882. After the Lafayette Place church was evacuated in 1887 prior to its destruction, a third church was erected at Second Avenue and 7th Street, "thoroughly equipped," as one guide said, "with reading-rooms, gymnasium, and all appliances for aggressive modern church work."

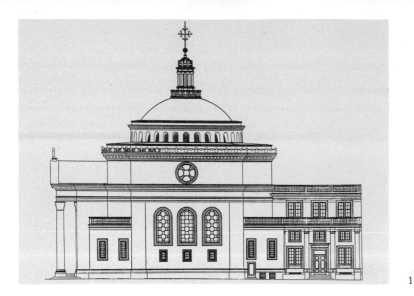

1

MADISON SQUARE PRESBYTERIAN CHURCH. McKim, Mead and White
designed a new Byzantine Madison Square Presbyterian Church (1) to take the place of the old Gothic
one at the southeast corner of Madison Avenue and 24th Street, which was in the way of the Metropolitan
Life Tower. The new church was completed in 1906 at the northeast corner of Madison Avenue and
24th Street (2); but in a few years that, too, was gone.

2

DR. TYNG'S CHURCH.   The Episcopal Church of the Holy Trinity was built by a parish founded in 1864 by the younger Stephen H. Tyng, a hardworking New York churchman. The congregation hired the Prague-born Leopold Eidlitz as architect, an exponent of a sort of Germanic Romanesque design. Dr. Tyng's Church, as the now demolished building was usually called, was completed in 1874 on the northeast corner of Madison Avenue and 42nd Street — just a block from the first Grand Central Station, which is seen in the distance (and on page 28).

TEMPLE EMANU-EL, 43RD STREET.   This photograph, one of fifty-seven wide angle pictures of as many blocks on Fifth Avenue, was taken by the Byron Company in 1924 but not rediscovered until 1962. The series was commissioned by a real estate firm to commemorate the 100th anniversary of Fifth Avenue, the first section of which was completed in 1824. The building on the right, at the northeast corner of 43rd Street, is Temple Emanu-El, long considered one of the finest synagogues in the world. By Leopold Eidlitz in association with Henry Fernbach, the building was erected in 1866–68. The temple was "Moorish," with Saracenic arches over columns inside, spanning a space for a congregation of nearly 2,000. But the land was enormously valuable. A year after this picture was made the congregation was looking for another home. The Eidlitz-Fernbach building was demolished in 1927, and a new temple, on 65th Street and Fifth Avenue, was dedicated in 1930.

150

ST. JOHN'S CHAPEL. St. John's (1), a church worthy of rank with St. Paul's, was built by the vestrymen of Trinity parish in 1803. It was the masterpiece of John McComb, Jr., who later improved Castle Clinton (page 96) and collaborated on the New York City Hall. Here his collaborator

1

was his brother Isaac. The interior of the church was as fine as the Georgian St. Paul's, which in fact St. John's much resembled (2). The chancel was built in 1857 by Richard M. Upjohn. The chapel spire, of hewn oak and with a town clock, rose above the surrounding buildings, 214½ feet high. A Corinthian portico with four large columns of sandstone stood in front.

In the first years of the church a park was laid out before it, bounded by Varick, Beach, Hudson and Laight Streets and called Hudson Square, or St. John's Park. It was improved and fenced by the property owners who had built substantial houses around it. The photograph of St. John's Park (3), made about the time of the Civil War, shows it shortly before it was sold by the city to Commodore Vanderbilt. In 1867 he covered the entire site with four acres of train sidings and the Hudson River Railroad Freight Depot (4). Virtually none of the neighborhood residents remained. A writer in the '90s found St. John's Chapel the only church within a great area, surrounded by factories and tenements. The church and a few houses adjacent remained standing until 1918, when the city carelessly destroyed them while widening Varick Street.

3

4

MOVEMENT.

The vitality of cities depends first of all on the richness of their communications networks, for it is through these that encounters are made to permit shopping, recreation, working, and every other urban activity. Before the telephone revolutionized communications, it was necessary to travel to communicate instantly, and some kind of movement between people and goods still accounts for most urban contacts. It follows that many different kinds of transportation should be encouraged in order to facilitate as many opportunities as possible for diverse communication. Not only is this a requirement to make a place dynamic and interesting, but it also provides for much smoother operations in the daily life of the city, eliminating bottlenecks by providing intentional plurality and overlapping of function. A man on West 59th Street knows he can get to the theater on West 45th Street within twenty minutes, because he can either walk, or take a taxi, subway, bus, or he can get there in a combination of ways. If only one of these alternatives were available, he would probably need to allow himself much more time because of congestion or the possibility of unforeseen delay.

While some means of transportation (such as the horse and cart) have obviously become obsolete, others are permitted to wither when they could and should be actively sustained. Pedestrian walks have been systematically eliminated whenever they have vied for space with motor traffic. The Triborough Bridge and Tunnel Authority decided that the new Verrazano–Narrows Bridge did not need a pedestrian walk; one can therefore never stop on the bridge to see a stunning view of the harbor. The same agency widened the roadway on the Whitestone Bridge and eliminated the walk shown in the photograph on the opposite page. The Port of New York Authority left the originally planned rapid transit line off the second deck of the George Washington Bridge.

Communications possibilities not only ought to be obtainable, but should be *seen* to be obtainable. There should be no secret about the route taken by a bus, the identification of a taxi (New York is very good about this), the location of a railroad station or subway stop or phone booth. Great communications centers and movement terminals require explicit architecture. The city's clarity and operation are disabled when the forms and patterns of diverse movement are destroyed.

The Bronx-Whitestone Bridge spans the East River, linking the Bronx with Queens. It was built in 1937–39, by Othmar H. Ammann and Allston Dana, engineers, and Aymar Embury II, architect, with provision for pedestrian and vehicular traffic. Precautionary wind bracing was subsequently added to the edges of the deck, thus obstructing the view off the bridge, and sidewalks were eliminated to provide three motor lanes in each direction.

154

TRAIN SHED. The British first put railroads to use. Most of the great British railroad stations were built in the 1850s and '60s, and while none of them was as notably palatial as New York's later Pennsylvania Station, they in fact usually followed a different plan principle. The ticket office and waiting rooms were in a masonry front. Connected, but often entirely unrelated to it architecturally (and sometimes not even designed by architects), was the train shed. This was a great canopy of iron and glass; at its best — as in York and Paddington — taking the form of vaults that curved not only in section but in plan, so the effect was like walking within a coiled spring.

The 1871 Grand Central train shed, shown here, was inspired by such stations. John B. Snook was the architect, Isaac C. Buckhout the engineer. The cast and wrought iron arches, spanning 200 feet, were far loftier than those of most great stations in Britain. Though the train shed inevitably had to be removed in 1906 to make way for functional changes (see pages 28 and 31), the clarity of its great cylindrical form was never surpassed in later building.

156

DOUBLE-DECKER BUS.   Ease of access to public transportation — now being recommended for cities in the form of monorails, electric taxis and minibuses — was available in New York when public transportation was the only kind that most people could get. From about 1890 to 1920, open-sided trolleys were widely used which could be boarded from anywhere along their sides whenever they went slowly. The trolleys' need for a non-driving conductor made their manpower requirements high, and the last vanished from the Central Park West line in the '30s.

The double-decker bus was a public vehicle which abided longer. In its motorized form it was run by the Fifth Avenue Coach Company from 1907 until 1946. The double-deckers allowed a sensible saving of space on the crowded avenue, and the ones with open tops were magnificent in all kinds of weather. Like the open-sided trolleys, the old double-deckers also had a conductor for fares, but if they were boarded between stops, at least it was more likely to be from the sidewalk. According to the Fifth Avenue Association's book *Fifty Years on Fifth*, they were abandoned for the very reason they should be reinstituted: "Because of the interminable rides taken by the bewitched."

HUDSON FERRIES.　　Before the Holland Tunnel was built, there were thirty-eight Manhattan ferry lines, besides upstream and freight lines.　Ferries were the only means of communication
between Manhattan and the west.　The first Hoboken ferry was established in 1774, and after the introduction of steam ferryboats to New York in 1814, that Hudson crossing became the major one.　Access
to New Jersey was available at eleven ferry points below 24th Street.　The number of crossing points
was a great convenience for passengers, a transit versatility unmatched by the motor vehicle routes that
put the ferries out of business.　This photograph shows the Hoboken ferry terminal, run by the Erie–
Lackawanna Railroad, at the foot of 23rd Street.

SUBWAY ENTRANCES.   Subways have proved the most practical, most serviceable — and most nerve-deadening — way of moving around New York. Since the (now abandoned) elegant City Hall station of the IRT was built in 1904, it seems that no further attempt was ever made to build a system for use by people. Apart from the plainness of the stations and passageways, the complex networks, frequent stairs, dead-end alcoves, lack of passenger direction planning, variety of structural devices, poor choices of materials, noise of equipment, and lack of signs make the New York subway perhaps the worst piece of public design work in the civilized world — one obvious reason why it is often vandal-ridden and dangerous as well.

Just about the only parts of the subway system that appear to have been created by a human being, the iron and glass subway entrances that protected descending passengers from wind and emerging ones from rain, are being removed and will all be gone by 1967.

COMMERCE.

Commercial buildings provide the best case for urban conservation, as distinguished from preservation. Since they have no important function other than efficient operation for profit, it would be very expensive, even if practical, for anyone to subsidize *preservation* in commerce once operations had become uneconomical. Yet if key commercial buildings and districts were treated as long-term *conservation* problems, normal government powers (such as taxation, zoning, development of communications improvements) could be used to aid their continuing efficient use.

Many lost commercial buildings in New York have been destroyed because management needed more space or better communications and consequently moved out, with the result that specialized and elegant buildings left behind found no willing users. The New York Herald building was one such example (see page 169). Such losses could be kept to a minimum with an active municipal commercial development program that had conservation of urban form as one of its avowed aims.

Another frequent cause of unnecessary demolition occurs primarily in rental rather than self-tenanted properties. Buildings are torn down to be replaced by new buildings of greater floor area, or by another building type that currently provides higher returns. This happened to the old German Savings Bank building (see page 165). If it is actually against the general public welfare for such changes to take place, existing use and bulk ought to be defended with zoning laws. These laws are now on the books, but permissive interpretations in the past have rarely limited a developer's goals. Better than compulsory government powers would be tax advantages, rigged to encourage building on underdeveloped sites rather than rebuilding on well developed ones. This would not only create a broader base for taxation; the appearance and good use of efficient business districts could be also thereby maintained.

Older commercial buildings are frequently simpler to alter than technically sophisticated new ones. A conservation attitude would encourage the maintenance of old buildings and keep them fit for continuing use. Rather than limit new construction, this would lead to more healthy growth and change.

Pier of the French Line. This interior — showing pointed arch timber truss construction — was probably at the pier of the Compagnie Générale Transatlantique when it was located on West Street between Horatio and Jane Streets. The French Line piers are now uptown, and this early structure has been replaced by a steel-framed pier.

WESTERN UNION.   The now vanished Western Union building was built in 1873–75 at
Broadway and Dey Street, George B. Post the architect. The Western Union and the New York Tribune
buildings have been called the first skyscrapers, since both were the earliest ordinary commercial structures to incorporate elevators. The ten-story, 230-foot Western Union building was also one of the first
buildings to face the stylistic problem of what to do with all that slenderness. For the time being, the
solution seemed to be to make the top third a rather splendid Renaissance palace.
Overhead wire networks grew thicker and thicker until the late '80s, when most were put underground
in conduits.

BANK OF AMERICA.   The innovation of the elevator (and later the steel skeleton) caused many property owners to look less fondly at their properties, particularly if they were on very valuable downtown sites. Many landmarks of commerce were scrapped in favor of added floor space. One such was the building shown above, the 1835 Bank of America at the northwest corner of Wall and William Streets. In 1889 it was replaced by a nine-story successor that not only provided more room for the bank, but had offices to rent. In the new elevator buildings every floor was equally accessible, a revolutionary development in real estate as well as architecture, since rental possibilities suddenly reached up beyond the lowest two levels.

163

WORTH STREET.   The block of Worth Street between Broadway and Church Street once contained a row of cast-iron front commercial buildings, the finest such group east of St. Louis. Most were built around 1869 by the architect Griffith Thomas as dry-goods warehouses, but they soon became the New York textile center. When the garment district developed uptown the immense wholesale activity of the block was stilled, with only a few fabric houses remaining there. Most of the block was razed in 1963 for a parking lot.

THE GERMAN SAVINGS BANK. The thin elements, sharp detail, and high relief possible with the use of cast-iron elements made for a new kind of light but vigorous architectural expression that affected even conventional construction, and large glass areas were attempted as well in masonry buildings such as the German Savings Bank, at the southeast corner of 14th Street and Fourth Avenue. It was built in 1870–72, with Henry Fernbach the architect. An apartment house now occupies the site

ECCENTRIC MILL WORKS. James Bogardus (1800–1874), watchmaker, inventor builder of towers (see page 93), "Architect in Iron" as he called himself in his 1858 booklet *Cast-Iron Buildings — Their Construction and Advantages*, keeps New York from second place to either Chicago or London in the invention and development of iron in building. He devised and popularized a prefabricated system of cast-iron elements for factory buildings which are the ancestors of Lever and Seagram. Bogardus was a system-builder who saw no limit to the use of cast iron. Only one of his buildings remains in New York (see page 214). This print shows the eccentric grinding mill manufactory he built for his own use, which had a complete metal frame, including prefabricated piers, columns, beams and wall panels. It was completed in 1849 at the corner of Centre and Duane Streets in only weeks of assembly time, and was disassembled again ten years later when Duane Street was widened — a now-vanished landmark of modern architecture. Bogardus's later conception of an advanced structure for the 1853 New York World's Fair involving a circular catenary chain-supported roof was rejected in favor of the imitative Crystal Palace (see pages 182–83).

HARPER'S, FRANKLIN SQUARE.   Bogardus's most elaborate commission was executed in 1854 for the Harper & Brothers building at 331 Pearl Street in Franklin Square, which was razed in 1920. A fire had completely destroyed the publisher's plant in 1853, and even though the fatal weakness of iron construction in a fire was not then well understood, Bogardus and John B. Corlies, the collaborating architect, did a thorough job of reducing danger on the new building.

It was not a complete iron fabrication system as the Eccentric Mill Works had been, since it used masonry in the facade and in load bearing. But Bogardus continued to demonstrate his inventive imagination in the girders he designed for Harper's. Cast iron, while strong in compression, is crystalline and consequently very brittle. If long cast-iron beams or girders had any flaw in them, they cracked open from the bottom. The girders Bogardus provided were of cast iron shaped like arches, with rods along the bottom of wrought iron, a far more elastic material. Soon wrought-iron rolling mills were turning out full-sized structural members, but Bogardus's inventiveness foreshadowed the use of extra-strength steels in parts of modern buildings.

THE A. T. STEWART STORE.   John W. Kellum was one of the many architects who worked in cast iron in the '50s. His 1859 department store for A. T. Stewart east of Broadway between 9th and 10th Streets (later half of Wanamaker's, and the scene of a spectacular fire during demolition in 1956) was a complete iron frame structure manufactured by the Cornell Iron Works, one of the most extensive buildings ever done in that material, and one of the simplest in appearance.

1

2

THE NEW YORK HERALD BUILDING.   McKim, Mead and White designed
this Venetian palazzo for James Gordon Bennett. It was erected at Broadway and 35th Street (Herald
Square) in 1893. The delicate building was stuffed with printing presses which could be admired from
the arcades. Its famous clock is the only part of the public-spirited design that survives — now at the
south end of the square.

1

2

THE TIMES TOWER.   The Times Tower (1) was begun in 1903 in what was then Longacre Square. Completed in 1905, it was twenty-five stories high, and New York's second tallest structure.   It was also known as "the second Flatiron building," because of its shape — both buildings being characteristic of Broadway's acute-angle intersection with avenues.   The *New York Times* outgrew the building in 1913, but owned it until 1961. The new owner had it stripped down to bare steel (3) and remodeled by the architectural descendants of the original designers, Cyrus L. W. Eidlitz and Andrew C. McKenzie. The bland effacement reopened in 1966.

Is its alteration really a loss? One thing worth remembering is that the building was a popular landmark for its entire life — very much so when it was built, but also years later, as picture postcards showed (2); it was clearly one of the

three or four New York buildings instantly recognizable to people all over the world. The building was not in itself remarkable — just another try at giving a skyscraper some fashion. The site had much to do with the Times Tower's conspicuousness. The *Times* chose it wisely, as the *Herald* had chosen their site elsewhere, a few years before. Both newspapers located buildings prominently in what was in each case the center of town at the time, where newspaper offices deserve to be (they are fortunate in having their names still associated with those central places). Seen this way, the Times Tower's new face and new use is clearly no improvement. What is now at No. 1 Times Square, on the Great White Way, at the Crossroads of the World, is not an important New York building, but only another piece of outdoor advertising — a junior-executive monument self-dedicated to "the show business of big business."

NEW YORK TELEPHONE COMPANY. Only the ceiling remains in this shrine of instant communication, the Booth Room at the New York Telephone Company building. The directory altar and the booths like confessionals have given way to advanced equipment. The building, at 140 West Street, dates from 1923–26; McKenzie, Voorhees and Gmelin, architects.

CHRYSLER OBSERVATION LOUNGE.   Now housing television transmission equipment is the shell of what once was the Observation Lounge in the Chrysler building — the logically expressionistic summit of New York's most winning skyscraper. The vivid building by William Van Alen at Lexington Avenue and 42nd Street (where Edward Trumbull's lobby still remains) was completed in 1930.

BLACK, STARR & FROST. Like the Times Tower, the Black, Starr & Frost building (at the southwest corner of Fifth Avenue and 48th Street) has been transformed by the placement of a flashy new skin over the old skeleton. Unlike the Times Tower, the architecture destroyed in 1964 by the new owner, a bank on the make, was one of the best small business buildings in the city. It was designed in 1912 by Carrère and Hastings, architects of the New York Public Library.

LORD & TAYLOR, BROADWAY.   The Lord & Taylor department store occupied this now substantially altered building from 1872 to 1902, the fifth Manhattan location of the company. (The fourth was on Broadway and Grand Street.) This store was on the southwest corner of Broadway and 20th Street, and had an iron frame and a new steam elevator. The iron window walls of the building with their great areas of glass indicate how retail clothing was still something to be examined in the daylight.

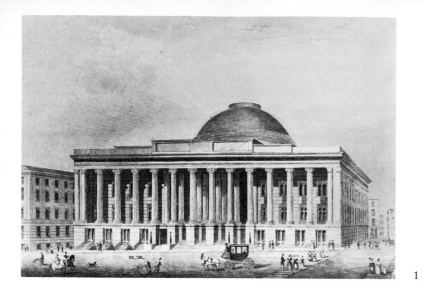

1

55 WALL STREET.   Isaiah Rogers built the Merchants Exchange (1) in 1836–42, on the site of an earlier one. It was distinguished by its Ionic colonnade and an eighty-foot dome. In 1863, the building became the Custom House, and the First National City Bank acquired it in 1899. By 1909, the bank had added four more stories by McKim, Mead and White. It had another giant order, Corinthian this time, piled over the sixteen Ionic columns — an original and staggering sight that can still be seen. Inside, an efficient pneumatic message system was installed (2). The new floors enclosed but at first did not cut off the original dome. Modifications were carried out to make the room a single banking floor (3), now altered and considerably diminished.

3

Very few institutional buildings on valuable land can be so efficient that they remain in successful use for 125 years. But this building's state of steady change through its history justifies calling it "lost," since it has come far from its greatest days — a fact that ought to be considered in the Preservation Commission's allowance for further change, now that 55 Wall Street has become a designated Landmark.

2

1

MARKETS AND SHOPS.   Retail marketing would undoubtedly account for the greatest turnover of money in New York, if it was considered a single industry. Shops therefore ought to have prominence in a book about a city, but the process of cash-and-carry is apparently so simple that its architecture is usually purely ornamental, besides being almost always ephemeral. A few to remember:
The vanished food market at Broadway and 95th Street (1), which somewhat resembled the earlier New Central Market, a free-enterprise grocery with rented stalls at Broadway and 48th Street, built in 1868 . . .

2

3

The Windsor Arcade (2), designed by Charles I. Berg for Elbridge Gerry, on the east side of Fifth Avenue between 46th and 47th Streets; New York's most famous and elaborate shopping block until it disappeared by halves in 1912 and 1920 . . . William Lamb's 1933–34 retail block at Madison Avenue, 59th to 60th Streets (3), where reflections of the International Style once could be discerned in the glass . . . And, of course, there are some shops in a retail chain's constant style that are remembered because they still seem to be around (4).

4

PUBLIC AMUSEMENTS.

The financial failures of New York's Freedomland and the 1964 World's Fair appear to indicate that this kind of outdoor amusement is no longer being supported by the public in numbers that justify the expense of their maintenance. Actually, the grand spectacle of middle-class society in general attendance at amusement parks and similar public recreation — the image of the Crystal Palace, the Columbian Exposition, the scenes painted by Manet, Seurat and Renoir — began to fade at the end of the 19th century. And this rapt public seems to have markedly diminished around the time when automobiles began to allow many people the privilege of seeking private amusements.

Yet it would be worth learning whether the automobile, as well as the television set and other vehicles of individual fancy, were really the cause of the decline of public amusements. Even after driving out into the natural landscape, most people today still seek the society of others. Picnic areas and comfortably tamed camping places are by far the most popular parts of national parks.

The reason for the decline of organized public amusements may have something to do with the modern status of children, and the place they have at the center of family life. If zoos, amusement parks and fairs — even museums — are seen as being principally for the entertainment of children, then what these have to offer adults must necessarily be limited. Old photographs of Luna Park and Dreamland have scarcely any children in them at all. The amusement parks were designed to be at their most magnificent at night. They were romantic environments where courtships could be forthrightly conducted. The Tunnels of Love were built for serious couples, not for bored children. Fun was a dignified adult proposition, and the present decline of public amusements may be principally the result of self-limitations — a diminished view of our own capacities.

The Coney Island Elephant was a well-known New York curiosity. Other houses shaped like elephants had been built in Europe. The beast's impressive architectural dimensions were noted on the reverse side of this advertising card. The Elephant, now long gone, also appears in a photo of Coney Island in King's 1893 *Handbook of New York City.*

THE CRYSTAL PALACE.   The site of the New York Exhibition of 1853 was at Sixth
Avenue and 42nd Street, just west of the Croton Reservoir. Schemes for an exhibition building submitted
by Leopold Eidlitz and Bogardus & Hoppin were passed over in favor of an octagonal structure of iron
and glass with a dome, by the architects George Carstensen and Charles Gildemeister (1). The Crystal
Palace design was derivative of Paxton's 1851 London pavilion in name and materials, and both were
also prefabricated, repetitive, and technologically precise. (The aerial view was made from the Latting

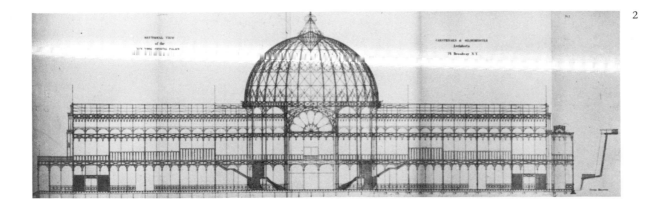

Observatory, a tall, braced-timber tower with an early steam elevator, built as a public attraction during the World's Fair. The tower stood across 42nd Street to the north, and burned down in 1856.)

Carstensen and Gildemeister's design (2) was perhaps unnecessarily complex and formally derivative, but for those very reasons it demanded sophisticated detailing and a great variety of framing techniques (3). While all this made it less interesting architecturally than the Crystal Palace in London, it was a widely publicized lesson to American designers in the versatile use of iron — a lesson soon transferred by others to theater roofs, skylights, train sheds, and blocks of iron buildings. There was a nationwide enthusiasm for the Crystal Palace and the possibilities of iron construction. Bogardus even thought iron buildings could be built ten miles high. Iron was a perfect material: strong, cheap, not easily rusted when cast, fireproof — or so it was thought. In fact, iron is drastically weakened in a high temperature.

The awful truth about iron and glass buildings became clear when the combustible contents of the Crystal Palace caught fire on October 5, 1858. The fire twisted and collapsed the entire structure in an incredible fifteen minutes' time. Soon after, the destruction of the Crystal Palace was being as widely vaunted as its creation (4).

3   4

CRYSTAL PALACE
RELICS !

Mrs. RICHARDSON, of New York, (who was one of the unfortunate persons burnt out by the fire that destroyed the Crystal Palace,) by permission of the MAYOR OF NEW YORK, and of JOHN H. WHITE, Esq., Crystal Palace Receiver, obtained a number of curiosities very valuable for a cabinet, produced by the melting of the Building, and articles on exhibition, which she now offers to visitors at the FAIR AT PALACE GARDEN, as interesting souvenirs of all that remains of the finest building ever erected in America—a building made entirely of glass and iron, except the floors—and supposed to be almost wholly free from danger of fire; yet, it was utterly destroyed on the 5th of October, 1858, in fifteen minutes' time. The evidence of the immense heat will be seen in the articles now offered for sale, as well worthy the attention of the curious.

An interesting memorial of the great Crystal Palace Exhibition, is found in Mrs. RICHARDSON'S collection of Relics, which is on exhibition in the 3d floor. They consist of vitrified masses of glass, metals, &c., showing the intense heat which prevailed in the building at the time of its destruction.—THE SUN, Oct. 11.

Wynkoop, Hallenbeck & Thomas, Printers, 113 Fulton Street, N. Y.

1

2

RECREATION PIERS. The New York Regional Plan of 1929–31, a proposal that was not timid about its new highway plans for Manhattan, nevertheless roundly disowned the West Side Highway. The planners found fault with it because its location cut people off from the Hudson River and made the development of new riverfront recreation facilities most difficult. The influence of the Regional Plan Association's comment was presumably modest, because the alignment of the new East River Drive soon repeated the mistake on the other side of the island. Since the penny-wise New York commissioners who laid out the 1811 grid of streets had reasoned that the city did not need many parks because of New York's healthful relationship with its river edges, one finds that official planning has, in its history, both turned people toward the water and then stopped them from getting there. This double bind may one day have to be resolved by means of expensive landfill and redevelopment.

Before Manhattan's girdling highways were built, and before pollution devitalized the rivers, recreation piers provided some of New York's most pleasant public playgrounds. The idea of recreation piers was a natural one in Coney Island, where the now vanished Iron Pier at Brighton Beach was so popular that it was featured in stereoscopic views (1, 2, 3). It was an I-shaped construction with elaborate pavilions at both ends, and in addition to dining

4

and strolling, it was the landing place for the Iron Steamboats which brought holidaymakers there.

There were once six officially designated recreation piers in Manhattan, and one in Brooklyn — "Play Piers" as Jacob Riis called them, or "Roof Gardens" as the users did (4, 5). The first opened at the foot of East 3rd Street in 1897 at the instigation of Riis, and its enormous success led to others on the East River at 24th Street and 112th Street, and on the Hudson at Barrow Street (part of the Christopher Street Ferry slip), 50th Street and 129th Street. They were opened from 8:00 A.M. until 10:30 P.M. from June to November, and were crowded most of the day with children and later with parents and young couples, cool in the evening fresh river air.

5

STEEPLECHASE, THE FUNNY PLACE.   Steeplechase Park, created in 1897 as the first of the great Coney Island amusement parks, closed for good in 1964, the twenty-five acre site having been sold for a housing project. Steeplechase was "The Funny Place," as signboards used to say (over the painted face of the founder George C. Tilyou wreathed in an incredible smile). The amusement park got its name from one of its most famous rides — the wooden steeplechase horses that started together

1

at the top of a long system of track. Riders would mount the horses, each of which straddled one of the parallel rails. When the brake was removed, all the horses would start at once, zooming up and down the course that circled the pavilion and looped in and out through its walls (1, right). The building itself was a simple steel frame (2) housing, among other diversions, Coney Island's second most important Elephant (see page 181). The most popular attraction was the extra-cost Parachute Jump (1, left), a great draw at the time of the 1939 World's Fair. The park was once destroyed by fire in 1907, but was rebuilt in 1908. Mr. Tilyou meanwhile invited the public in to see the ruins for ten cents a look.

2

1

DREAMLAND. The fantasy architecture of pleasure grounds might serve as a profitable source of information on the aspirations and imaginary adventures of a society. Once ordinary formalistic pre-conceptions are swept aside in the spirit of fun, design seems to turn directly toward the stuff of dreams inspired by contemporary ideals. (The Rhineland gardens of Schloss Schwetzingen had recreational "ruins" and a "mosque" in 1776, long before aspirations toward the Picturesque had made any inroads in serious German architecture.) Just as the amusement parks of today present as public fantasies strong images of space travel and scientific exploration, those of sixty years ago showed public fantasies common

3

to that time. New York had them in two prevailing moods: the Apollonian Luna Park, and the Dionysian Dreamland.

In Dreamland, long vanished, a culture that admired the work of the National Sculpture Society in Beaux-Arts triumphal arches found the lost world of legend — in forms not like Art Nouveau, as they might have been, but in decoration almost as original; and sometimes, as at the entrance facade, strangely Sullivanian (2). Stucco ornament illustrated fancies from Wagner (3) to *kitsch* (1). At night, bulbs would light the dragons' wings.

190

LUNA PARK.   A mood and style at Coney Island which was far from spooky gorges — although with a prevailing fantasy of its own — was at Luna Park, beautiful Luna Park that the visiting Maxim Gorki called "fabulous beyond conceiving." Thompson and Dundy opened it in 1903, and the things it showed that had been borrowed from Chicago had nothing to do with Louis Sullivan. The great spectacle was the White City itself of the 1893 World's Fair, condensed (1) but also dematerialized (2). Like the White City (and the still extant Tivoli Gardens in Copenhagen), Luna Park was European, sophisticated, somehow noble; dignified fun. Before it burned down, it was a pleasure garden where ordinary people could savor amusements in good society, as at Vauxhall, Cremorne or the Bal Masqué.

WORLD'S FAIR 1939. Returning from the 1937 Paris Exposition, Grover Whalen, president of the New York World's Fair Corporation, was optimistic on the subject of peace. Assuming that his prediction of the state of the world remained correct, he envisaged the opening of the World's Fair on April 30, 1939 on the theme of "Building the World of Tomorrow." World's fairs and national expositions present a situation where architecture is supposed to express national ambitions and ideals. In fact, those held since 1851, when international fairs were reinvented for post-classical times, have been basically celebrations of *laissez-faire* commerce and perpetually nineteenth-century ideas of trade and progress. In a depression year, Lewis Mumford called the notion of a fair a "completely tedious and unconvincing belief in the triumph of modern industry. The less said about *that* today, the better."

But the biggest and costliest of all fairs up until that time opened as scheduled, and perhaps even many of the nation's 13,000,000 unemployed passed through the turnstiles where the pre-pop art National Cash Register building, designed by Walter Dorwin Teague (1), busily counted the customers. Once on the reclaimed land of Flushing Meadows, where 6,700,000 cubic yards of garbage had been moved and graded in 190 days, visitors could see and orient themselves from the Trylon and Perisphere (2), the theme centerpiece by Wallace K. Harrison and J. André Fouilhoux. This was a 700 foot high tapered pillar (the "finite") and a 200 foot steel-framed globe (the "infinite" — or was it the other way around?). Between the two was the Helicline: a ramp. At night, moving colored marble patterns were projected on the globe. Color was in fact one of the significant design preoccupations of the Fair, where the Board of Design (which made sure, among other things, that state pavilions were stylistically correct in deriving from Georgian, French or Spanish influence) had Julian E. Garnsey, for the sake of good taste, select 499 colors available to architects.

In the spirit of the Big Cash Register, there were pavilions for Cosmetics (a giant lady's powder box), RCA (a radio tube), Gas (grid points on a range surrounding a flame), and the Continental Baking Company (a doughnut). In the midst of all this highly finite design soared the infinite Finnish Pavilion (3, 4), Alvar Aalto the architect, fresh from attaining his new world reputation in the 1937 Paris Exposition. Aalto's three-story undulating screen repeated the vertical stick idea that was common to his 1937 and 1938 pavilions in Paris and Lapua, Finland. While the representation being made in New York was not specifically of forestry and agriculture, the theme of his historic design at Lapua, the technical performance clearly evoked some associations with Finnish lakes and forests. The physical impact was apparently

1

2

even more evocative. Siegfried Giedion found that "The cantilever of the upper stories, which so intensifies the impression of hovering movement, provides room for a concentrated display of objects. The outstanding feature is the new modeling of inner space that is involved in this experiment, which to many still appears rude and almost barbaric." The loss of the Finnish Pavilion at the end of the Fair is comparable to the loss of Mies van der Rohe's German Pavilion in Barcelona, built ten years earlier. Both were irreplaceable landmarks of modern architecture.

Next to the Finnish Pavilion, some of the few other good works at the 1939 Fair seem small losses, if otherwise deserving of credit. The Danish unit of the Hall of Nations (5) had some of the same crisp design as the

4

Museum of Modern Art (see page 109), finished the same year. The French Pavilion (6) had lots of character, and even style, though transitional.

The New York 1939 Fair first showed to the world some lasting innovations, if not any as revolutionary as the use of neon lighting in the Chicago Fair of 1933. Some of these were the exhibits that moved to the audience (and vice versa), the effective and wide use of mirrors, and the telephone exhibit, where free long-distance calls could be made before an appreciative audience. What these novelties had in common was the participating crowd, the people who were there to see. In retrospect, the Board of Design's layout for the Fair (7) was unexceptionable and the Fair's architectural mean was probably higher than that of Manhattan, but the discovery that people were what exhibits

5   6

were for was the most significant contribution. In the *Architectural Record* in 1940, a writer looked back and thought that this proved "an influence toward democracy more powerful than many a columned building." A more distant view adds the ideas of the Road of Tomorrow to the Fair's prescience — only twenty years after, the highway had already changed the nation even more than anyone had dared predict. Probably most people remembered best General Motors and Ford, and Pierre Labatut's fireworks displays — "the nearest approach to chaos that man can contrive for purposes of sheer entertainment." Before the Fair closed, Grover Whelan found man approaching chaos for other purposes.

7

WORLD'S FAIR 1964.   The Board of Design of the 1939 World's Fair saw to it that the improved fairgrounds would be able to remain as a park. The site plan, the work of many men, had been designed with a view to Lewis Mumford's suggestion that an ideal scheme was one giving the visitor an immediate understanding of the whole exposition. The result was a rigid pattern where axes crossed more or less concentric rings. Even on the ground, it was a paper plan; absolutely two-dimensional despite the opportunities presented by all the earth-moving that had to be done. But once the Trylon and Perisphere formed a center to the ring avenues and radial avenues, the plan at least heeded Mumford. The central symbol was as directional as a north arrow, and told the visitor where he was.

When the site was used again for the 1964 World's Fair (after a term as a neglected park, and for a while as the United Nations location) the theme symbol again occupied the center, but the Unisphere was just the opposite of a directional guide. A banal and sculpturally crude globe based on an armillary sphere, the skeleton structure of hoops looked and worked exactly like the celestial globes it was patterned after. It was something to look through; and from any radial avenue, the symbol looked the same and failed to be a guide.

In the sense that the Unisphere never satisfied a useful purpose, it was truly symbolic of the 1964 Fair. A dismally unimaginative and uncomprehending management caused the resignation of its consulting architects and financial advisors. Most foreign countries stayed officially out because the Bureau of International Expositions had withheld recognition. The exposition run by Robert Moses and his staff hardly bore any relation to its avowed theme, "Peace Through Understanding." In fact, as a representation of international, national, or even civic ideals and ambitions, it seemed so bankrupt that its generous support with public funds was virtually a public embarrassment. Amid all the crassness and chaos, the inference was — as Yale Professor Vincent Scully described it in a review for *Life* magazine — that this was all accurate, it was America, that Mr. Moses had our number.

1

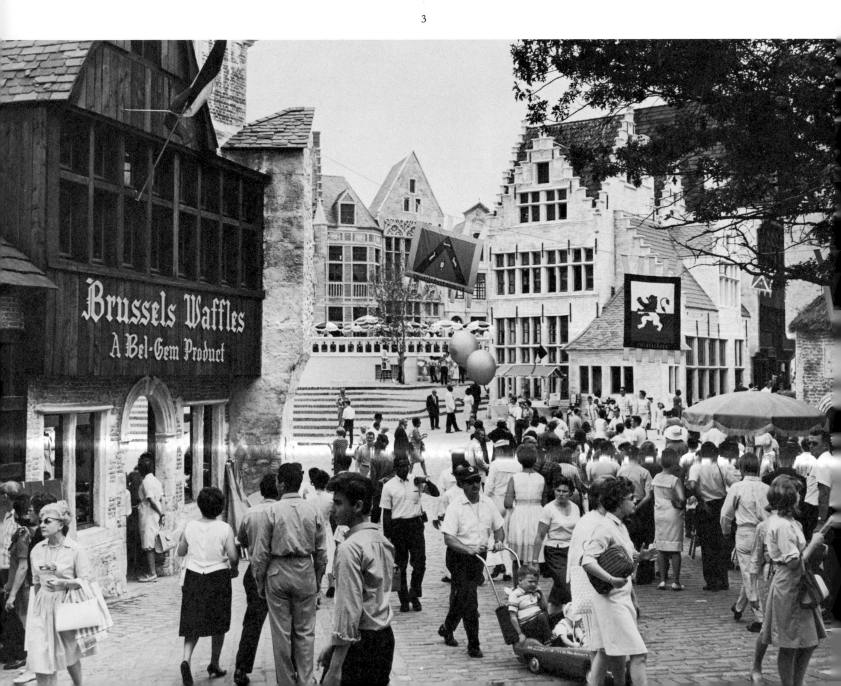

4

Within the organizational shambles, many individual works were witless and savage, the average architectural accomplishment being far lower than that of 1939. There were, of course, Gulliverian exhibits, such as the U.S. Rubber tire (1), which George Washington Gale Ferris would hardly recognize as related to his trim invention of 1893. The most enthusiastic attendance was at the Belgian Village (2, 3) — an artificial bit of Tiny Europe, where the popularity of its make-believe streets only indicated how incoherent the rest of the Fair was.

What the Fair really had to offer (with one exception) was not architecture; at least not in the old sense of the word — not buildings. It offered exhibits, usually wholly internal presentations, some of them excellent. The pretentious shapes given the pavilions seldom had any relation to what went on inside. The trouble was that most architects had continued to design competing fancy forms, when in 1964, the whole nature of World's Fair spectacles had changed. Many pavilions exhibited film experiments, moving displays, moving audiences. Apart from the subject matter (generally unworthy of the show), some exceptional experiences were offered at the IBM, General Motors and Johnson Wax pavilions. Some of the buildings most praised (the Spanish Pavilion, the Japanese Pavilion with its carved stonework) were really throwbacks: formal, inexpressive, pretty buildings — not good ones. The U.S. Pavilion, frequently the highest praised, was in this sense one of the poorest. The best thing the Fair had, however, was a distinguished work of architecture which would have been outstanding in any company. The New York State Pavilion (included here for discussion, though a $750,000 conversion expenditure may rescue it) somehow captured, without belittling, the spirit of public assembly for entertainment; a walk-in, walk-out canopy connected to some observations towers (4, 5); for all its decoration and high style, truly simple and truly an example of Mies van der Rohe's pronouncement, "less is more." Architect Philip Johnson and Governor Nelson Rockefeller deserve the credit for seeing through this affirmation of people's importance and noble character, amid denial and doubt.

5

LANDMARKS IN DANGER.

According to the New York Landmarks Preservation Law, a landmark is specifically "any improvement which has a special character or special historical or aesthetic interest or value as part of the development, heritage or cultural characteristics of the city, state or nation and which has been designated as a landmark . . ." But beyond the legal definition, there is the general meaning of the word: a conspicuous object in the landscape, a point-reference, a simply defined physical object. This suggests that a landmark is specifically concerned with the place where it exists; furthermore, that its external appearance is its most significant feature.

Neither of these things may be true about some of the most valuable architectural elements of New York. Many of the buildings that reveal aspects of the truth about the city in terms of its "development, heritage or cultural characteristics" may be exactly the ones that have been left behind as the city developed, and no longer have anything to do with their immediate environment. Saving them is not a matter of the conservation of vital urban elements, but the preservation of remains. In other cases, it may be true that buildings worth saving are innocuous in external appearance, but their interiors — or their functional uses — make them essential city elements. Certain shops, restaurants and banks are like this, and their public accessibility makes them part of the experience of New York. Preservation legislation should also be applied to outstanding examples of these non-landmarks. It would also seem that any definition of architectural importance which does not include the significance of *use* is a limited one.

The photographs that appear in this section are therefore not only of landmarks in the Preservation Law sense; yet the word "landmark" is now so firmly ingrained that it seems as well to use it in describing all things worth saving. It is important enough to note again that this can be done through preservation or conservation; that the Preservation Law does only a limited part of the job; and that conservation may be much more difficult, if more rewarding in the long run.

These pictures obviously can be no more than some representative examples of valuable New York places reported to be in danger at the time of writing. It is to be hoped that some of these reports, like the rumors of Mark Twain's death, were exaggerated. The Landmarks Commission continues to designate buildings for preservation, and this may have already saved several shown here. As for those already gone, they at least are hereby mourned, along with the rest of the vast body of good building that has become lost New York.

Friends Meeting House, 144 East 20th Street. The congregation has been reunited with the Quaker Meeting at Stuyvesant Square, and the property has been sold to developers. The building — by King & Kellum, 1859–60 — occupies an important position on the south side of Gramercy Park, and has a fine meeting hall with balcony inside. It has been designated a Landmark, and private efforts to save it may be successful.

203

MADISON SQUARE PARK.   "Diana's little wooded park," as Madison Square was sometimes called when the statue of Diana looked down from the tower of the old Garden (1), is being strongly recommended as the site of an underground garage. This has been proposed by the present New York traffic commissioner, and is supported by the Fifth Avenue Association. While the project is now at a standstill, plans have been drawn for the garage and it might be revived at any time.

This proposal would mean the destruction of most of the park's 300 trees (2), since the garage would pre-empt the space required for their roots. It would also require a ventilation and exhaust system visible on the surface. San Francisco, which the traffic commissioner points to as "progressive" in undertaking similar programs, has in fact ruined most of its downtown parks and plazas by turning them into concrete lids for garages, and replacing trees and grass with industrial materials.

Besides being a threat to the park, the proposal serves to encourage more cars to come into New York, further snarling traffic and short-circuiting public transportation. It is also a proposal unrelated to any planning scheme, and would by its piecemeal approach sacrifice long-range public benefit to what is thought to be immediate commercial advantage.

In any case, nearby unpublicized parking lots are now not fully utilized during business hours (3).

1

2

3

1

BROOME AND GRAND STREETS. The story of the
Lower Manhattan Expressway proposals will one day undoubtedly be written,
since it would be greatly instructive — in the history of early regional
planning and city government — as a lesson on how vital decisions were once
made. The highway was first suggested around 1930, when the country
needed roads to everywhere and cars for everyone. During the postwar
federal highway program, cities and Authorities lined up to get a share of the
90% of project costs underwritten by the national government. The over-
worked Mr. Robert Moses, as "Coordinator of Federal-State-City Arterial
Projects," began his heavy support of the Lower Manhattan Expressway in
1941, and with the mayor's approval at last his in 1965, started to acquire
property along the dream route of the '30s. By March, 1966, with a less

2

obliging municipal administration demanding modern plans showing concern for the fabric of the city, the Expressway was said to be definitely out. But until that full story about the Expressway is written, it might be best not to speculate on Mr. Moses's comeback powers, and instead look at some of the outstanding architecture in the way of his proposal.

The cleared area required would include practically all of Broome Street, with many entrance and exit ramps cutting back into parallel streets as well. Typical of Broome Street, which the Landmarks Commission has said "contains the best cast-iron architecture still preserved in the United States," is No. 433 (1), an anonymous gem of about 1865. At 462 Broadway, corner of Grand, is a cast-iron building (2) erected in 1879 for George Bliss and Frederick H. Cossitt as a dry goods warehouse. Both buildings continue to be in good use.

E. V. HAUGHWOUT & CO.   The Lower Manhattan Expressway's most historic proposed victim is the department store put up for E. V. Haughwout & Company, which has been called "the Parthenon of New York's iron age." Now designated as a Landmark, it is used as a commercial building, at the northeast corner of Broome Street and Broadway. Haughwout had the first passenger elevator in the United States, installed by Elisha Graves Otis in 1857, when the building was built. The cast-iron construction and skin — a handsome exterior still in virtually perfect condition (2) — was fabricated by Daniel Badger, who was Bogardus's rival and whose company was the other big New York

1

architectural ironworks. John P. Gaynor was the architect perceptive enough to engage the services of Otis and Badger.

In the latter half of the 19th century, Broome Street became devoted to wholesale business, with firms making and supplying everything from buttons to carriages. Most of the buildings from that time can still be seen (1), their low rents and flexible layouts now serving as "incubators" (as an economic report of the area put it) for new Manhattan industries.

2

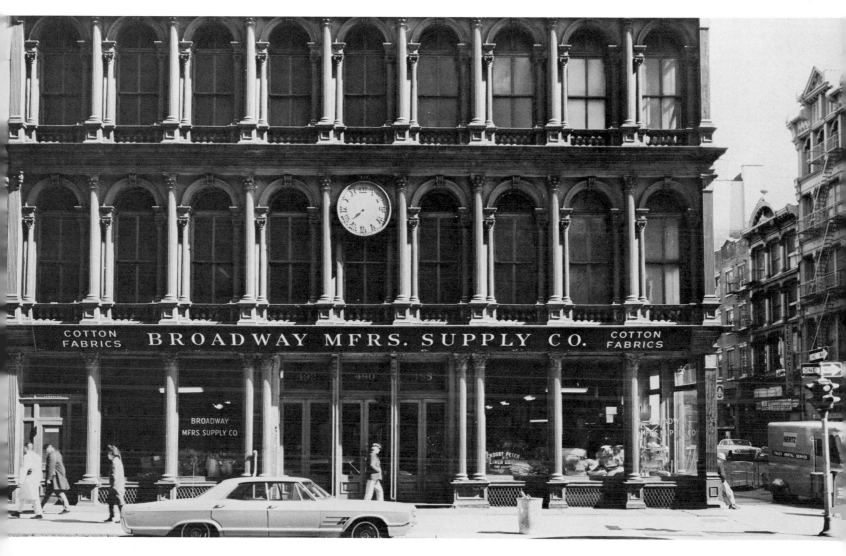

210

2

SINGER AT PRINCE STREET. Possibly in the way of one of the exit or entrance ramps of the Lower Manhattan Expressway is this small building (1, center — considered a skyscraper at the time) built for the Singer Sewing Machine Company by Ernest Flagg. The structure is L-shaped, fronting at 561 Broadway and 88 Prince Street, and was begun in 1902 and completed two years later.

The building is remarkable for its use of bold materials which clearly articulate the structural form. This is not merely the "expression of the structure," but in fact a new ornament based on essential properties required by use. The wrought-iron railings and brackets guard the sun-screen balconies. The building frame is sheathed with terra cotta (2), a very efficient fireproofing for steel, its decoration clearly marked to avoid the connotation of self-supporting masonry (the panels are orange, their surrounds blue). The glass down to the floor has an exceptionally large area, and because arranged in casements, a window type most satisfactory when used beneath overhangs, ventilation is flexibly provided without great cost or heavy sash detailing. Altogether, Ernest Flagg put together a pioneer building, one that looked ahead at least fifty years.

1

2

SINGER TOWER.   Ernest Flagg's impressive design of the small Singer building led to his commission for the forty-seven-story Singer Tower at 149 Broadway, the tallest building in the world for eighteen months (until the Metropolitan Life Tower was built). When finished in 1908, the tower element which soared above the lower section — a building begun in earlier stages — had an unparalleled slenderness (1) and was braced by crossed diagonals in the corners, a kind of support against wind pressure now commonly used in steel buildings. Flagg's tower and ideas about height may have influenced New York's zoning ordinance of 1916.

As is most evident in its spectacular lobby of colored marble, bronze, and glass-saucer domes (2), the manner of the Singer Tower is more clearly Beaux-Arts than the Singer building on Prince Street. The interior would not be out of place in a René Clair film. But its basic association seems to be with the client's product: that ornamental, practical, beautiful turn-of-century Singer sewing machine. The building's present owner, the U.S. Steel Corporation, may tear it down to clear the site for a new building.

212

BOGARDUS LOFT BUILDING.*   In 1849, James Bogardus finished this four-story row of storehouses for Edgar H. Laing, some time before his own Eccentric Mill Works (see page 166) was completed. The Laing Stores — erected in two months — is not a complete iron structure such as Bogardus and Daniel Badger were fabricating later in their separate works. It is valuable because it has a historically early ironclad exterior, and is the only known complete building by Bogardus now surviving in New York. It still stands at the northwest corner of Washington and Murray Streets, but has lost most of its original applied cast-iron ornament. Its present state of neglect and its location in an Urban Renewal area show it to be in danger.

---

* The interiors are now slated for demolition, but with the cooperation of other city departments, the Landmarks Preservation Commission has succeeded in saving most of the iron facades. They will be taken down and preserved for re-erection on a future site.

THE ZIEGFELD THEATER.*   This theater was designed in 1927 by Joseph Urban and Thomas W. Lamb. Urban's auditorium in the New School of Social Research on West 12th Street, and his Ziegfeld Theater, at the northwest corner of Sixth Avenue and 54th Street, are both echoes of the first great generation of the modern movement in architecture. The iconoclastic geometry of the New School auditorium, reminiscent of the work of Otto Wagner and Adolf Loos, is equalled by the classical expressionism — to give it a name — of the Ziegfeld facade.

The theater for the last several years has had occasional use as a television studio, but it has been long reported for redevelopment. Its unique value as a souvenir of an age, together with its fairly up-to-date stage facilities, make it a prime candidate for preservation as a Landmark.

---

* At last word the building and site have been sold to developers for $17,100,000, and demolition is in progress.

J. P. MORGAN RESIDENCE. The former house of John Pierpont Morgan, Jr., has been designated as a Landmark, and the question of its survival is a study in unsettled preservationism. The house (left in photo), at the southeast corner of Madison Avenue and 37th Street, was originally one of three large garden-surrounded brownstones erected in 1853 by Isaac Newton Phelps for himself and members of his family. It later became the property of the Morgan family, forming part of the block-long group which includes the Morgan Library (top right), built in 1906 by McKim, Mead and White, with a 1928 annex by Benjamin Wister Morris (lower right). Since 1945, the house has been owned by the Lutheran Church in America, which now wants to replace it with an office building to house its national headquarters. Since there seems no way to make the building provide a proper return for the owners under their demanded conditions, almost any kind of financial concession may be inadequate — a situation arising from an uncomfortably tight corner built into the Preservation Law.

The accident of ownership should not cause the house to fall because it is in the way of yet another office block. Midtown needs the ensemble of buildings the way it is, and the city should be prepared to buy the house outright if necessary — perhaps as a new home for the Public Library's rare books and manuscripts.

216

JACKSON SQUARE LIBRARY.   This library was one of the first ten branches of the New York Free Circulating Library, founded in 1880. The branch at 251 West 13th Street, Jackson Square, was built in 1887 after the design of Richard M. Hunt, was paid for by George W. Vanderbilt, and once bore his name. The library is a solid, unpretentious small building, designed and admirably suited for its function. It is in a good location for use, and though not at all monumental in character, is well placed at the east end of Horatio Street. The library currently serves the area from Christopher Street to 18th Street west of Fifth Avenue. It has a capacity of over 25,000 volumes, and had a circulation of almost 200,000 books in 1964, mostly among its area's population of 46,000 people.

As a result of a deal apparently made when the Public Library agreed to take over the Jefferson Market Courthouse as a library, the Jackson Square branch may be abandoned. Presumably the parties concerned were not considering the undoubted population increase in the West Village over the next few years or the residents' present and future extensive library use. It has been suggested that the Public Library convert the Jackson Square branch into a writers' studio, supplied only with reference books and desk space, similar to the Allen Room at the 42nd Street branch. A better plan would be to repair the building as required, make over the top floor into accessible stacks, and continue present operations regardless of improved facilities elsewhere. The Public Library claims there is a staff shortage and not enough library school graduates available to run the branch. If true, the community ought to be able to provide a solution, and the city should be prepared to help.

1

THE SEVENTH REGIMENT ARMORY.   Since the land belongs to the city and will revert to it if the Regiment ever ceases to exist, the privately-owned Seventh Regiment Armory (1 — top of center tower now gone) is in danger, and is the building most worth keeping among the armories now shaky because of National Guard reorganization.   Between Park and Lexington Avenues, 66th to 67th Streets, it was built in 1877–80 by Clinton and Russell, architects, and Charles MacDonald, engineer. MacDonald here adapted the structure of the train shed (see page 156) to building construction for the first time, in the armory's drill shed. The interiors are very fine, including the main staircase (2), Company rooms (3, M Company) with some ornament by Louis Comfort Tiffany, and — said to be wholly Tiffany's work — the Veterans' Room (4). It is one of the nation's best buildings of that decade.

4

2   3

1

ELLIS ISLAND.   The former (1892–1954) U.S. Immigration Station, Ellis Island, is included here not because its main building (2, left) is threatened — which it is — but rather because the island's entire usefulness is in jeopardy. Ellis Island (1) has been declared a National Shrine, and apparently will be all but cast in bronze in the plans proposed for it by the Department of the Interior and their architect, Philip Johnson. A giant cup-shaped monument will be built. The two main buildings on the island will be "stabilized" by being gutted and landscaped, just like Much Wenlock Priory in Shropshire — except that this is not a 14th century monastery, but in one case a utilitarian structure without even rubble value. The other, the old Administration Building by Boring & Tilton, architects, deserves a better fate.

Why turn all Manhattan's neighboring islands into isolated monumental parks? (There is a similar proposal abroad for Welfare Island.) The many islands of Venice, in contrast, have people living on them, individual characteristics, and individual character. "Nostalgia" is the word the architect associates with the Ellis Island project. A better memorial would be based on worthwhile "Use," such as the new university once recommended to be here. Single-use zoning is absurd for an island. Without any inhabitants planned for it, Ellis Island as proposed would be just desolate terrain every night, and all day, too, eight months of the year.

2

HALL OF RECORDS.   Besides City Hall, the best building in the group that constitutes the present municipal complex is the Hall of Records at the northwest corner of Chambers and Centre Streets. It was officially opened in 1911 and designed by John R. Thomas and Horgan & Slattery, with sculptural ornament by Henry K. Bush-Brown, Albert S. Weinert, and Philip Martiny. Plans for a new Civic Center have sometimes shown this building eliminated. One proposal has a tall sheer office block directly north of City Hall. This is not really a bad site since it would mean clearing away the ineptly designed County Courthouse of Tweed Ring notoriety which crowds City Hall, and whose classical facades are baffled by internal half-level height relationships. But the proposed giant office building's location in respect to the McComb and Mangin masterpiece is naively unsubtle, and belittling to City Hall.

A better solution for a new Civic Center would undoubtedly emerge if the city would clarify its objectives and use requirements, then announce an international competition for a comprehensive design — with hope of preserving the Hall of Records in effective relationship to new buildings, and of getting a municipal complex as good as recent government center plans for Boston and London.

CUSTOM HOUSE. Following the demolition of Government House south of Bowling Green (see page 91), the land was developed with six houses later occupied by the offices of large foreign steamship companies, and therefore known as Steamship Row. Congress ordered the land purchased for a modern Custom House, and after some opposition and litigation, the properties became available for redevelopment in 1899. Cass Gilbert, later architect of the Woolworth building (see pages 107, 108), designed the building, which was completed in 1907 with sculpture by Daniel Chester French. The Custom House that now stands at the end of the Broadway-Bowling Green loop (1) is an impressive building in the right place for an important public building. The real estate coup in which the government was persuaded to move customs operations to the new World Trade Center deprives the building of its major user and places it in

1

2

a danger not relieved by its being declared a Landmark. Moreover, it is unlikely that the new home for customs will have the kind of interiors Cass Gilbert provided, such as the main hall with murals by Reginald Marsh (2).

THE ASTOR HOTEL.   The loss of a splendid hotel like the Astor (now being replaced by an office building) is a matter for public concern in New York. The site was acquired in a single property deal, rather than expensively assembled bit by bit, and this explains why one of the most valuable buildings for blocks around is being torn down, instead of some of the shabby buildings nearby. The Astor deserved to survive for several reasons: it was one of the very best hotels in New York, it was in the midst of the theater district and had new offices growing up nearby, and it had some elegant interiors. Most of all — like the similarly doomed Vanderbilt and Sheraton-East hotels — it deserved conservation because the need for hotel accommodation will eventually have to be met with new construction elsewhere. It would have been sound civic economy to permit a fine hotel, significantly connected with the past, to remain where it belonged.

The Astor, on Broadway between 44th and 45th Streets, was designed by Clinton and Russell and completed in 1904, four years before the New York to Paris Automobile Race, shown at the start in the photo.

THE METROPOLITAN OPERA.   Here is the archetype of unjustified destruction in cities — a great public building at the disposal solely of its owner. The principal reason for the Broadway and 39th Street Metropolitan Opera House's demolition is that the Metropolitan Opera Association refused to spare it, fearing competition from another opera company using their old house. They sold the opera property years ago, with compulsory demolition written into the bill of sale, and also managed to convince the Landmarks Commission, the city council and some New York music critics that conservation of the old house would hurt opera in New York. Without Landmarks Commission support there was only *ad hoc* protest. The Met's officers successfully overwhelmed a clear city planning issue with a clamor of criticism and impudent claims (among them the demand for a triple payoff from citizens trying to buy back the building), while simultaneously posing as friends of art.

The important planning issue, never heard above Met president Bliss's *fortissimo*, was the question of where Official Culture should live: exclusively in a "center," or in the largest possible number of places in the city. New York badly needed the anchor of a cultural institution remaining below Times Square; now more than ever, it needs another opera theater to become a *Redoutensaal* or Glyndebourne, or, yes, perhaps even the rival home of a new Hammerstein's Manhattan Opera. In January 1967 the roof came off the 39th Street building which would have most adequately and economically served such a purpose.

1

2

The Met, usually with capacity audiences, "couldn't afford" competition, and New York "couldn't afford" anything but free-enterprise opera.

The opera house opened in 1883, defeating the rest of the field (see page 79); was rebuilt in 1893 after a fire, and got a new proscenium in 1905 (2). The auditorium (3) was changed to eliminate a tier of boxes in 1940. The architect of the once-dignified building (1) was Josiah Cleveland Cady; the rebuilt auditorium was by Carrère and Hastings.

3

SAILORS' SNUG HARBOR.   This range of buildings is over 400 feet wide, and the main
structures were the 1831–41 work of Martin E. Thompson, architect also of the New York Assay Office
whose facade is now at the Metropolitan Museum (see page 98).   On its site and in its previous solitude
it must have been magnificent, but there is now still something about the group that evokes recollections
beyond the Greek Revival, both in classical and American history.   A visit to New Brighton, Staten
Island, where these Landmark dormitories face out over Richmond Terrace, is well worth the excursion,
especially since they may not be there much longer.

Sailors' Snug Harbor was founded through the generosity of Captain Robert Richard Randall in 1801.
He bequeathed his large Manhattan farm, just above the site of Washington Square, for the establishment
of a home for retired sailors.   The institution's present trustees insist that rehabilitation of the buildings
on Staten Island is unfeasible (though many architects would disagree), and claim that there is no other
room on the forty-acre site for a new building.   Negotiations between the institution and the Landmarks
Commission are in progress but legal action seems probable.   Walter F. Pease, a Manhattan lawyer who
is chairman of the trustees, says the dormitory group "is not a museum and it does not have any historical
significance."

228

ILLUSTRATIONS AND SOURCES.

A description of the illustration is followed by the date it was made, when obtainable; and the maker (the photographer unless otherwise indicated), when known. The last listing is the source.
Midtown compass directions are conventionalized, with avenues considered to be running north-south.

THE URBAN SCENE AND PUBLIC PLACES.   22

37(7)	*Pennsylvania Station. Interior showing Train Concourse, looking northwest.* Courtesy Avery Architectural Library.
38(8)	*Pennsylvania Station. Interior of General Waiting Room, looking northwest during demolition.* 1963. Nathan Silver.
38(9)	*Pennsylvania Station. North Carriage Driveway, looking west during demolition.* 1963. Nathan Silver.
39(1)	*Central Park, between 102nd and 103rd Streets.* New York Public Library.
40(2)	*Central Park bandstand.* Courtesy Ware Memorial Library, Columbia University School of Architecture.
41(3)	*Central Park.* Byron. Museum of the City of New York.
42(1)	*Lower Fifth Avenue from atop Washington Arch, showing Brevoort Hotel (white building on right). Looking north.* Wurts Brothers.
43(2)	*Park Avenue between 50th and 51st Streets, showing Sheraton East Hotel (right, beyond St. Bartholomew's Church). Looking north.* Byron. New-York Historical Society.

PRIVATE GATHERING PLACES.   44

45	*The Panhellenic. Interior of tower lounge. Northeast corner First Avenue and 49th Street.* Private collection.
46	*Broadway Tabernacle interior. Broadway between Worth Street and Catherine Lane.* Engraving from *Frank Leslie's Illustrated Newspaper*, March 15, 1856. Author's collection.
47	*Niblo's Garden interior, northeast corner Broadway and Prince Street.* Ca. 1845. Watercolor by B. J. Harrison. Museum of the City of New York.
48	*German Winter Garden interior. 45 Bowery.* 1856. Watercolor by Fritz Meyer. Museum of the City of New York.
49	*Atlantic Garden interior. 50 Bowery between Bayard and Canal Streets.* Engraving from *Harper's Magazine*, April, 1871. New York Public Library.
50(1)	*Great Roman Hippodrome, between Madison and Fourth Avenues, 26th and 27th Streets, showing Leonard Jerome house (right). Looking north up Madison Avenue.* Courtesy Columbia University School of Architecture.
51(2)	*Madison Square Garden, between Madison and Fourth Avenues, 26th and 27th Streets, showing Leonard Jerome house (right). Looking northeast from Madison Square Park.* New-York Historical Society.
52(3)	*Madison Square Garden interior, showing cattle show.* 1895. Byron. Museum of the City of New York.
53(4)	*Madison Square Garden, looking southeast down Madison Avenue.* 1895. New-York Historical Society.
54(1)	*Tammany Hall interior. North side of 14th Street, between Third Avenue and Irving Place.* Color lithograph, 1888. Courtesy Cooper Union Museum Library.
55(2)	*Tammany Hall, showing Academy of Music (left). Looking northwest.* 1881? New-York Historical Society.
56(1)	*Broadmoor Restaurant interior. East 41st Street.* Ca. 1930. Samuel H. Gottscho.
56(2)	*Pennsylvania Station Dining Room interior.* Courtesy Avery Architectural Library.
57(3)	*Claremont Inn, Riverside Drive near 125th Street. Aerial view looking northwest.* Wurts Brothers.
58(4)	*Delmonico's, northeast corner Fifth Avenue and 44th Street. Looking northeast.* Wurts Brothers. Museum of the City of New York.
59(5)	*Central Park Casino interior, the Black and Gold Room. Central Park.* 1933. New York Public Library.
60(6)	*Crillon Restaurant, 15 East 48th Street.* Private collection.
61	*Canfield's Gambling House, interior showing Gaming Room. 5 East 44th Street.* Private collection.
62(1)	*Waldorf Hotel, interior of Turkish Salon. Northwest corner of Fifth Avenue and 33rd Street.* Private collection.
62(2)	*Waldorf-Astoria Hotel, interior of Peacock Alley. Between Fifth and Sixth Avenues, 33rd and 34th Streets.* Private collection.
63(3)	*Waldorf-Astoria Hotel. Looking southwest.* Ca. 1919. New-York Historical Society.

64(4)	*Manhattan Beach Hotel, Coney Island, Brooklyn, [illegible] Stereoscope photograph.* New-York Historical Society.
65(5)	*Grand View Hotel, Fort Hamilton, Brooklyn.* 1888. New-York Historical Society.
66(6)	*Park Avenue Hotel, Park Avenue between 32nd and 33rd Streets. Looking southwest.* From *Select New York*, published by Adolph Wittemann, 1889–90. Author's collection.
67(7)	*Murray Hill Hotel, Park Avenue between 40th and 41st Streets. Detail.* Ca. 1937. Berenice Abbott. Museum of the City of New York.
68(8)	*Astor House, Broadway between Vesey and Barclay Streets. Looking west.* Courtesy Columbia University School of Architecture.
68(9)	*Fifth Avenue Hotel, Fifth Avenue between 23rd and 24th Streets. Looking northwest.* Ca. 1885. Courtesy Columbia University School of Architecture.
69(10)	*Savoy Hotel, showing Bolkenhayn Apartments (right). East side of Fifth Avenue, between 58th and 59th Streets. Looking east.* Wurts Brothers. New York Public Library.
69(11)	*Ritz-Carlton Hotel, Madison Avenue and 46th Street. Looking west.* Courtesy Columbia University School of Architecture.
70(12)	*Ritz-Carlton Hotel interior.* Byron. Museum of the City of New York.
70(13)	*Ritz-Carlton Hotel interior.* Byron. Museum of the City of New York.
71(14)	*Buckingham Hotel, Fifth Avenue between 49th and 50th Streets. Looking northeast.* 1913. New-York Historical Society.
72(1)	*Center Theater, Rockefeller Center, Men's Smoking Room interior. Sixth Avenue between 48th and 49th Streets.* Private collection.
73(2)	*Center Theater auditorium interior.* 1932. Samuel H. Gottscho.
74(3)	*Park Theater interior. Park Row.* Woodcut by Lansing, 1805. New-York Historical Society.
75(4)	*Chatham Garden Theater interior. Chatham Street between Duane and Pearl Streets.* Lithograph from drawing by A. J. Davis. New-York Historical Society.
76(5)	*Broadway Athenaeum, east side of Broadway at Waverly Place. Looking southeast.* 1874. New-York Historical Society.
77(6)	*The Bowery (Thalia) Theater, 46 Bowery. Looking north.* 1914. New York Public Library.
78(7)	*Academy of Music, 14th Street between Third Avenue and Irving Place. Looking northeast.* New-York Historical Society.
79(8)	*Academy of Music auditorium interior.* Engraving from *Ballou's Pictorial Drawing-Room Companion*, ca. 1854. Author's collection.
80(9)	*Pike's (Grand) Opera House, northwest corner of Eighth Avenue and 23rd Street. Looking northwest?* 1937. Berenice Abbott. Museum of the City of New York.
80(10)	*Pike's (Grand) Opera House. Detail.* 1936. Berenice Abbott. Museum of the City of New York.
81(11)	*Théâtre Français (Civic Repertory), 14th Street west of Sixth Avenue.* 1936. Berenice Abbott. Museum of the City of New York.
82(12)	*The New Theater, Central Park West and 62nd Street. Looking southwest.* 1909. Frances B. Johnson.• Courtesy Columbia University School of Architecture.
82(13)	*The New Theater. Interior of Main Vestibule.* 1909. Frances B. Johnson. New York Public Library.
83(14)	*The New Theater. Interior of auditorium.* 1909. Frances B. Johnson. New York Public Library.
84(15)	*Loew's 72nd Street. South side of 72nd Street west of Third Avenue. Lobby interior.* Courtesy Loew's Theatres.
84(16)	*Loew's 72nd Street. Mezzanine Promenade interior.* Courtesy Loew's Theatres.
85(17)	*Loew's 72nd Street. Auditorium interior.* Courtesy Loew's Theatres.
86(18)	*Casino Theater, southeast corner of Broadway and 39th Street. Looking southeast.* From *Select New York*, published by Adolph Wittemann, 1889–90. Author's collection.
86(19)	*Fulton Theater.* Courtesy Columbia University School of Architecture.
87(20)	*Earl Carroll Theater. Lobby interior.* New York Public Library.

CIVIC ARCHITECTURE. 88

89	*The Croton Reservoir, Fifth Avenue from 40th to 42nd Streets. Looking southwest and showing the Hotel Bristol (right, demolished 1929).* Ca. 1893. H. N. Tiemann. Private collection.

PUBLIC AMUSEMENTS.   *180*

193(2)	*World's Fair 1939. General view on peak attendance day, showing Trylon and Perisphere.* Museum of the City of New York.
194(3)	*World's Fair 1939. Finnish Pavilion interior.* Ezra Stoller Associates.
195(4)	*World's Fair 1939. Finnish Pavilion interior.* Ezra Stoller Associates.
196(5)	*World's Fair 1939. Danish unit of the Hall of Nations.* Constance Hope Associates.
196(6)	*World's Fair 1939. French Pavilion interior.* Private collection.
196(7)	*World's Fair 1939. Aerial view.* Museum of the City of New York.
197(1)	*World's Fair 1964, Flushing Meadow Park, Queens. U.S. Rubber Corporation Ferris Wheel.* Copyright New York World's Fair 1964–1965 Corporation.
198(2)	*World's Fair 1964. Belgian Village, aerial view.* Copyright New York World's Fair 1964–1965 Corporation.
198(3)	*World's Fair 1964. Belgian Village.* Copyright New York World's Fair 1964–1965 Corporation.
199(4)	*World's Fair 1964. New York State Pavilion.* Copyright New York World's Fair 1964–1965 Corporation.
200(5)	*World's Fair 1964. New York State Pavilion, aerial view.* Copyright New York World's Fair 1964–1965 Corporation.

LANDMARKS IN DANGER. 201

203	*Friends Meeting House, 144 East 20th Street. Looking southeast from Gramercy Park.* 1965. Nathan Silver.
204(1)	*Madison Square Park. Looking northeast from Fifth Avenue and 23rd Street.* Winter 1910–1911. New-York Historical Society.
205(2)	*Madison Square Park. Near 26th Street, looking west.* 1965. Nathan Silver.
205(3)	*Madison Square Park, showing New York Supreme Court Appellate Division building (right). Looking west along 25th Street to Madison Avenue.* 1965. Nathan Silver.
206(1)	*Commercial building, 433 Broome Street. Looking southwest.* 1965. Nathan Silver.
207(2)	*Commercial building, 462 Broadway. Looking northeast along Grand Street.* 1965. Nathan Silver.
208(1)	*E. V. Haughwout & Company building, northeast corner Broadway and Broome Street. Looking northeast along Broome Street.* 1965. Nathan Silver.
209(2)	*E. V. Haughwout & Company building. Detail, looking east.* 1965. Nathan Silver.
210(1)	*Singer Building, 561 Broadway and 88 Prince Street. Looking southwest.* 1965. Nathan Silver.
211(2)	*Singer Building. Detail, looking west.* 1965. Nathan Silver.
212(1)	*Singer Tower, 149 Broadway. Looking southwest.* Courtesy Columbia University School of Architecture.
213(2)	*Singer Tower. Interior of lobby.* 1965. Nathan Silver.
214	*Laing Stores, northwest corner of Washington and Murray Streets. Looking northwest.* 1965. Nathan Silver.
215	*Ziegfeld Theater, northwest corner of Sixth Avenue and 54th Street. Looking northwest.* 1965. Nathan Silver.
216	*J. P. Morgan, Jr. house (left), showing Morgan Library (right top) and Library annex (right bottom). Southeast corner of Madison Avenue and 37th Street. Looking east from above.* Wurts Brothers.
217	*Jackson Square Library, 251 West 13th Street. Looking northeast from Jackson Square.* 1965. Nathan Silver.
218(1)	*Seventh Regiment Armory, between Park and Lexington Avenues, 66th and 67th Streets. Looking northeast. From Old New York, published by Adolph Wittemann 1889–90.* Author's collection.
218(2)	*Seventh Regiment Armory. Interior, showing main staircase.* Courtesy 107th Infantry Regiment, New York National Guard.
218(3)	*Seventh Regiment Armory. Interior of M Company room.* Courtesy 107th Infantry Regiment, New York National Guard.
219(4)	*Seventh Regiment Armory. Interior of Veterans' Room.* 1899. New York Public Library.
220(1)	*Ellis Island. Aerial view, looking northeast towards Manhattan.* 1940? New York Public Library.

236

221(2)	*Ellis Island, showing Administration Building (left). New York Public Library.*
222	*New York City Hall of Records, northwest corner of Chambers and Centre Streets. Looking north from City Hall Park.* 1965. Nathan Silver.
223(1)	*United States Custom House, Bowling Green and State Street. Looking southeast.* 1965. Nathan Silver.
224(2)	*United States Custom House, interior of main hall.* Courtesy General Services Administration, Public Buildings Service, U.S. Government.
225	*Astor Hotel, Broadway between 44th and 45th Streets. Showing start of New York to Paris Auto Race in Times Square, February 12, 1908. Looking northwest.* Byron. Museum of the City of New York.
226(1)	*Metropolitan Opera House, between Broadway and Seventh Avenue, 39th and 40th Streets. Looking northwest, up Broadway, showing Times Tower in distance.* Courtesy Metropolitan Opera Association.
227(2)	*Metropolitan Opera House. Interior, looking west, showing proscenium arch and old curtain.* Courtesy Metropolitan Opera Association.
227(3)	*Metropolitan Opera House. Interior, looking east, showing auditorium from stage.* Courtesy Metropolitan Opera Association.
228	*Sailors' Snug Harbor, Richmond Terrace, Staten Island.* New-York Historical Society.

INDEX.

NOTE: When more than one page reference follows an entry, the principal reference is italicized.

238